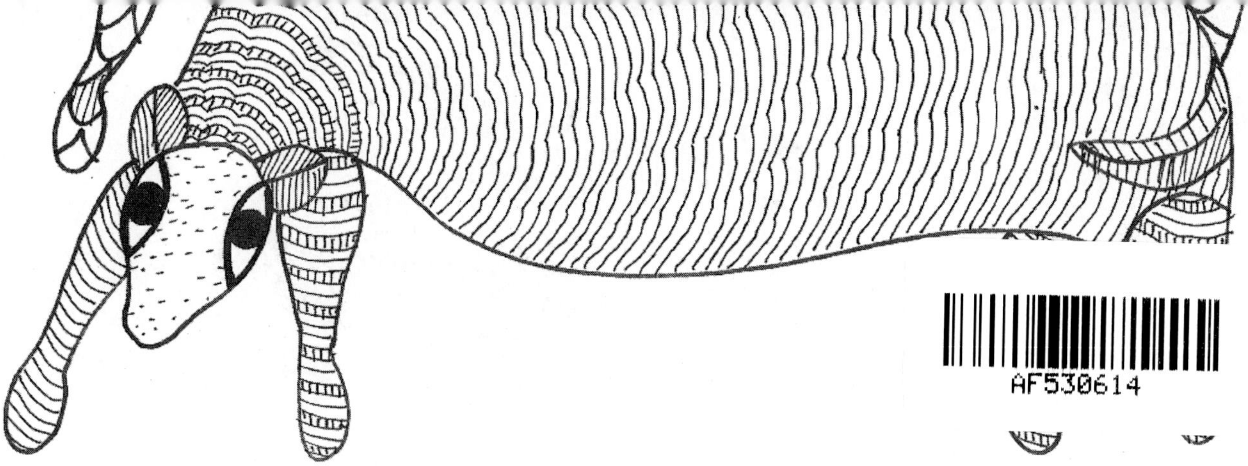

COLOURING INDIA

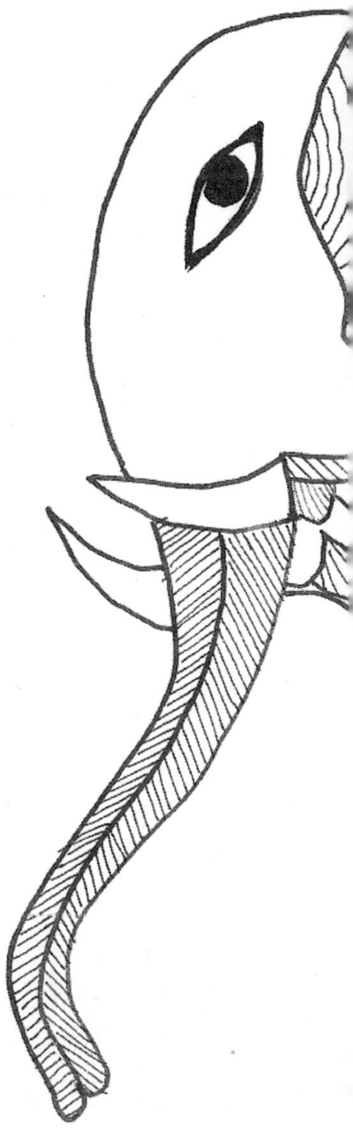

Joyous Colouring with Gond Art

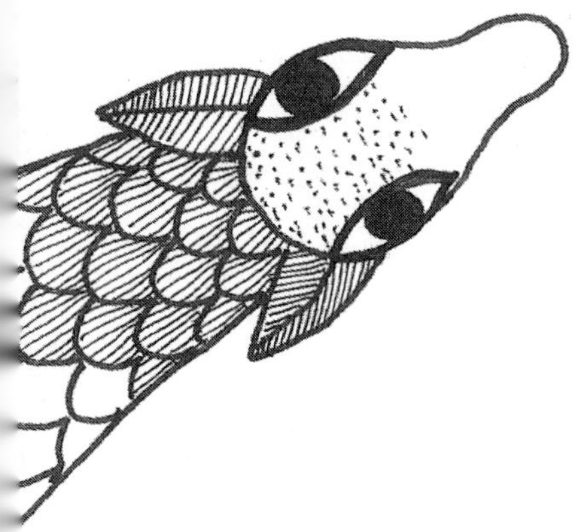

ILLUSTRATED BY
SUBHASH VYAM
EDITED BY BHAVI MEHTA

hachette INDIA

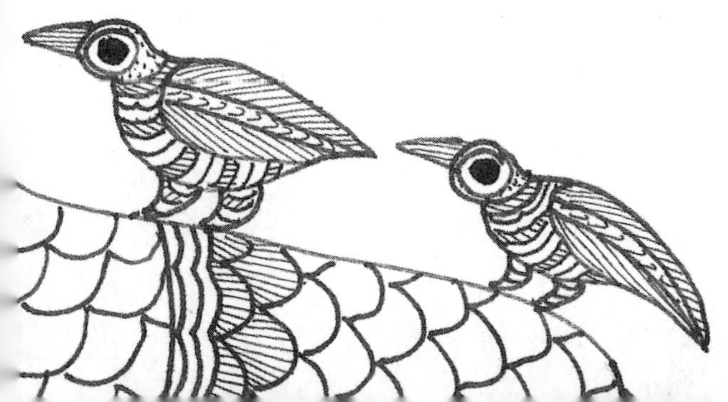

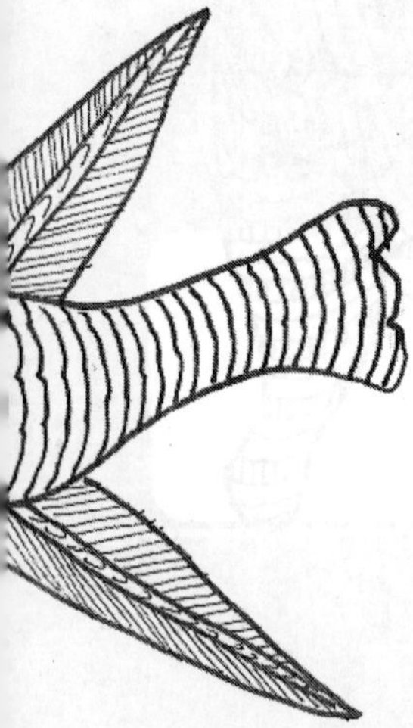

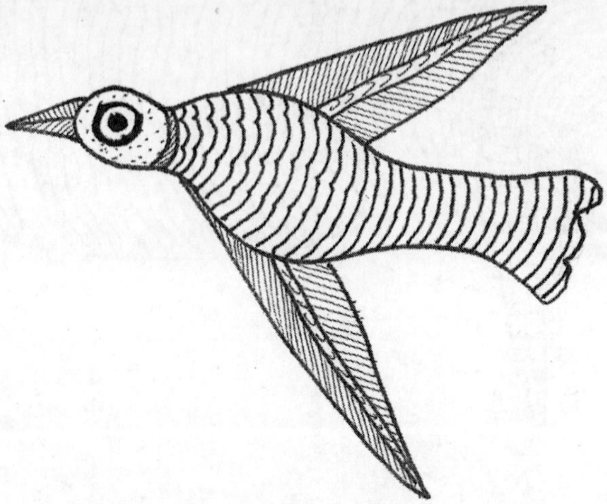

First published in 2016 by Hachette India
(Registered name: Hachette Book Publishing India Pvt. Ltd)
An Hachette UK company
www.hachetteindia.com

SRD

Cover and book design by Bhavi Mehta

ISBN 978-93-5195-160-5

Hachette Book Publishing India Pvt. Ltd
4th & 5th Floors, Corporate Centre,
Plot No. 94, Sector 44, Gurgaon - 122003, India

Printed and bound in India by
Manipal Technologies Limited, Manipal

MIX
Paper from responsible sources
FSC www.fsc.org FSC™ C043100

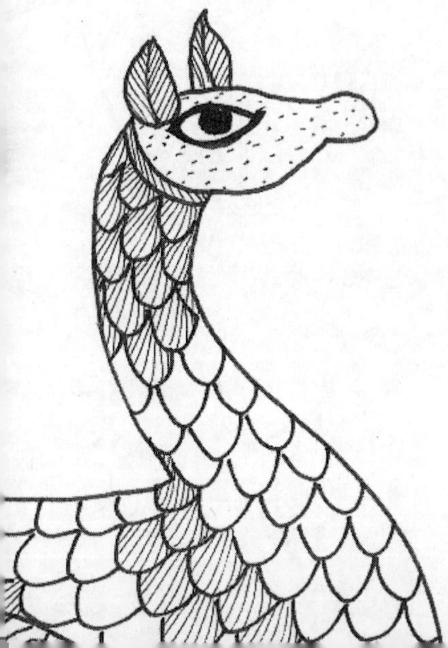

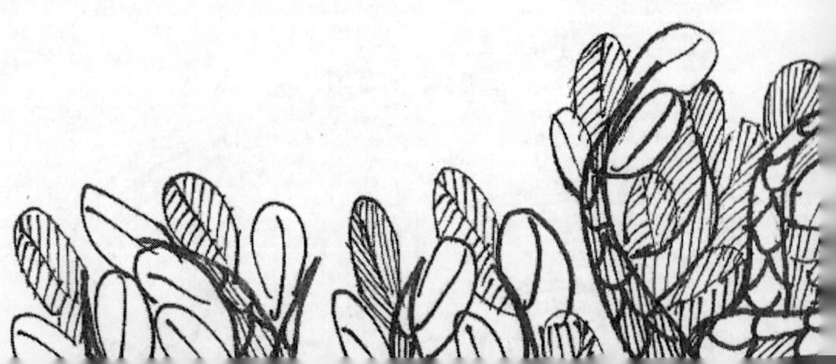

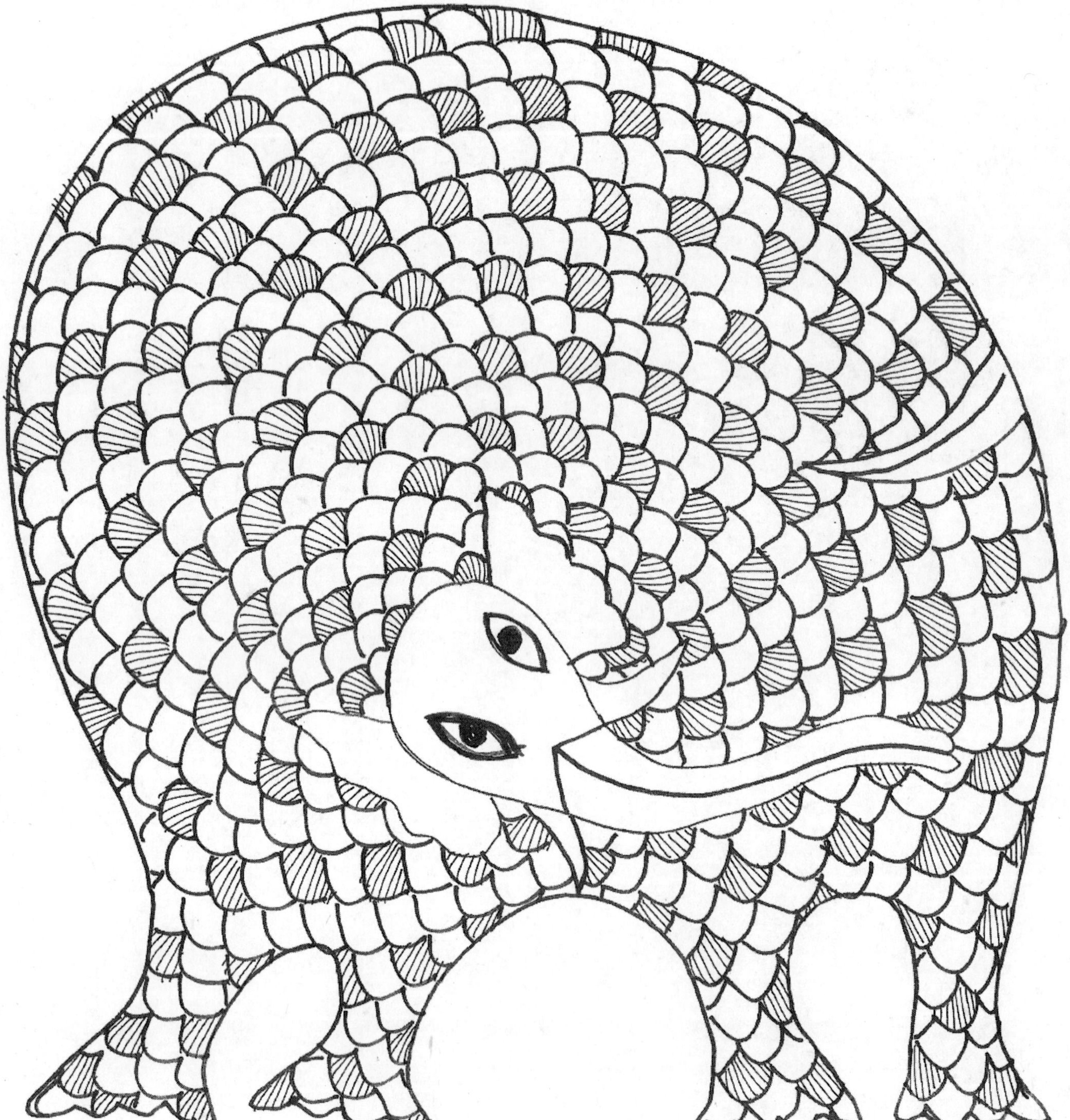

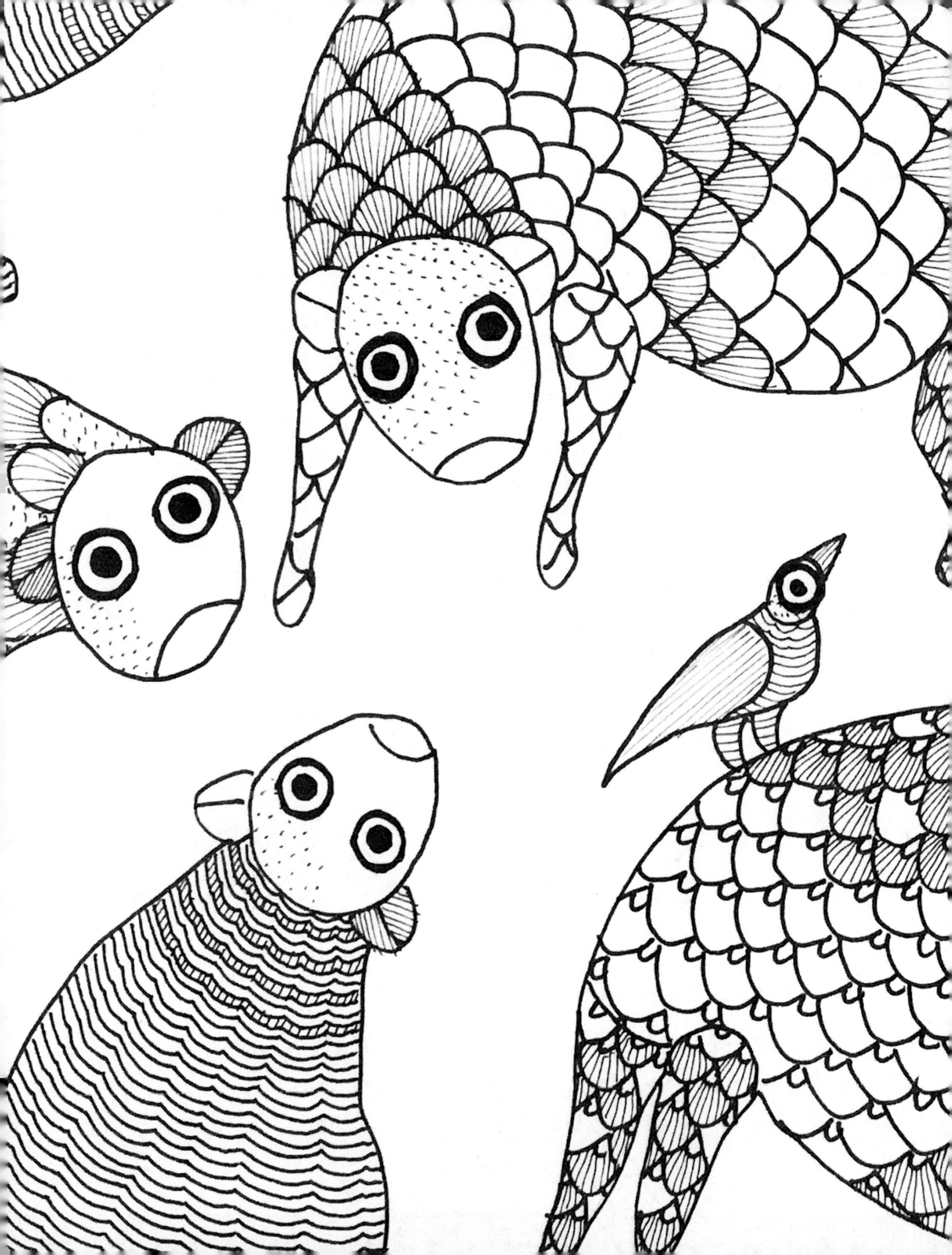

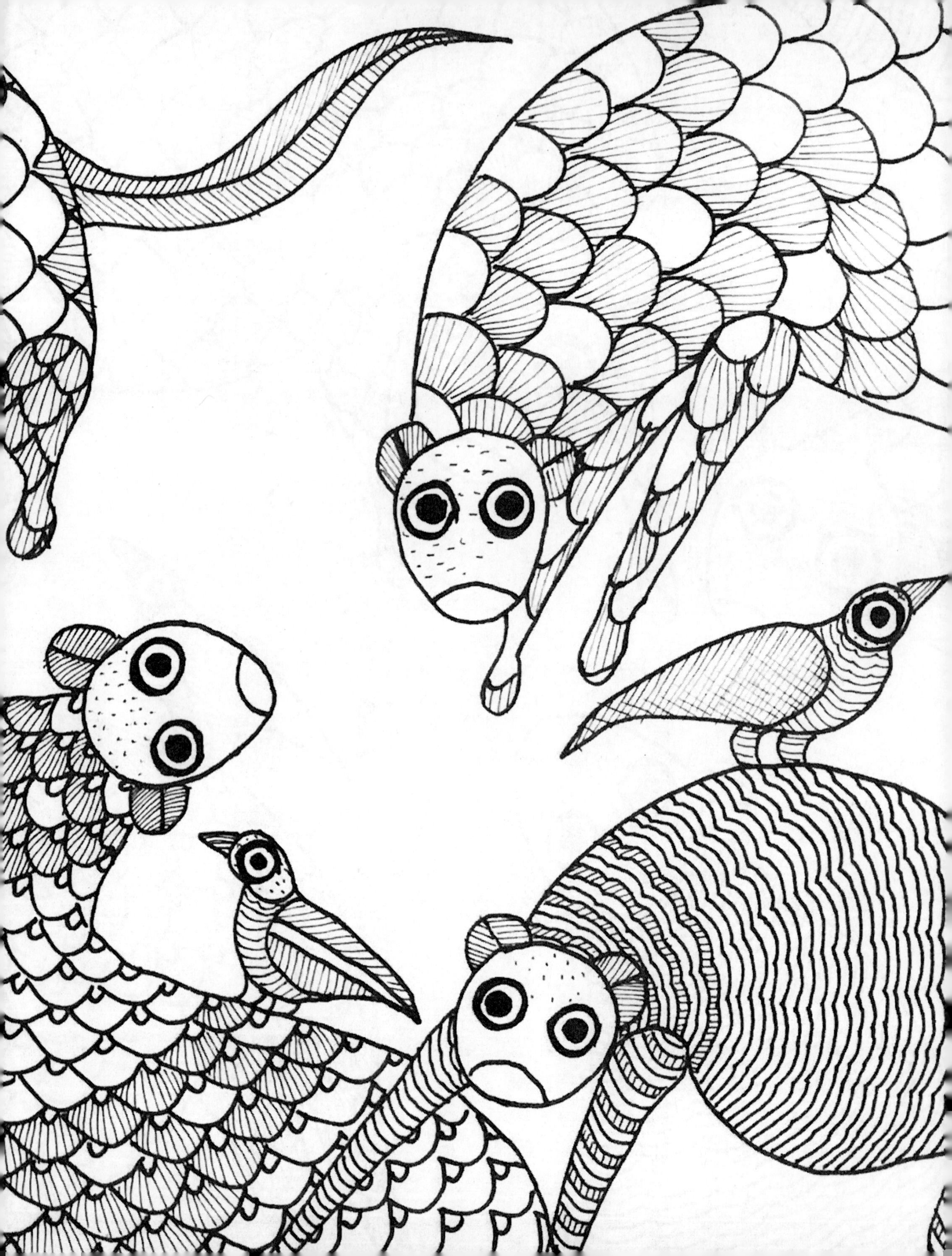

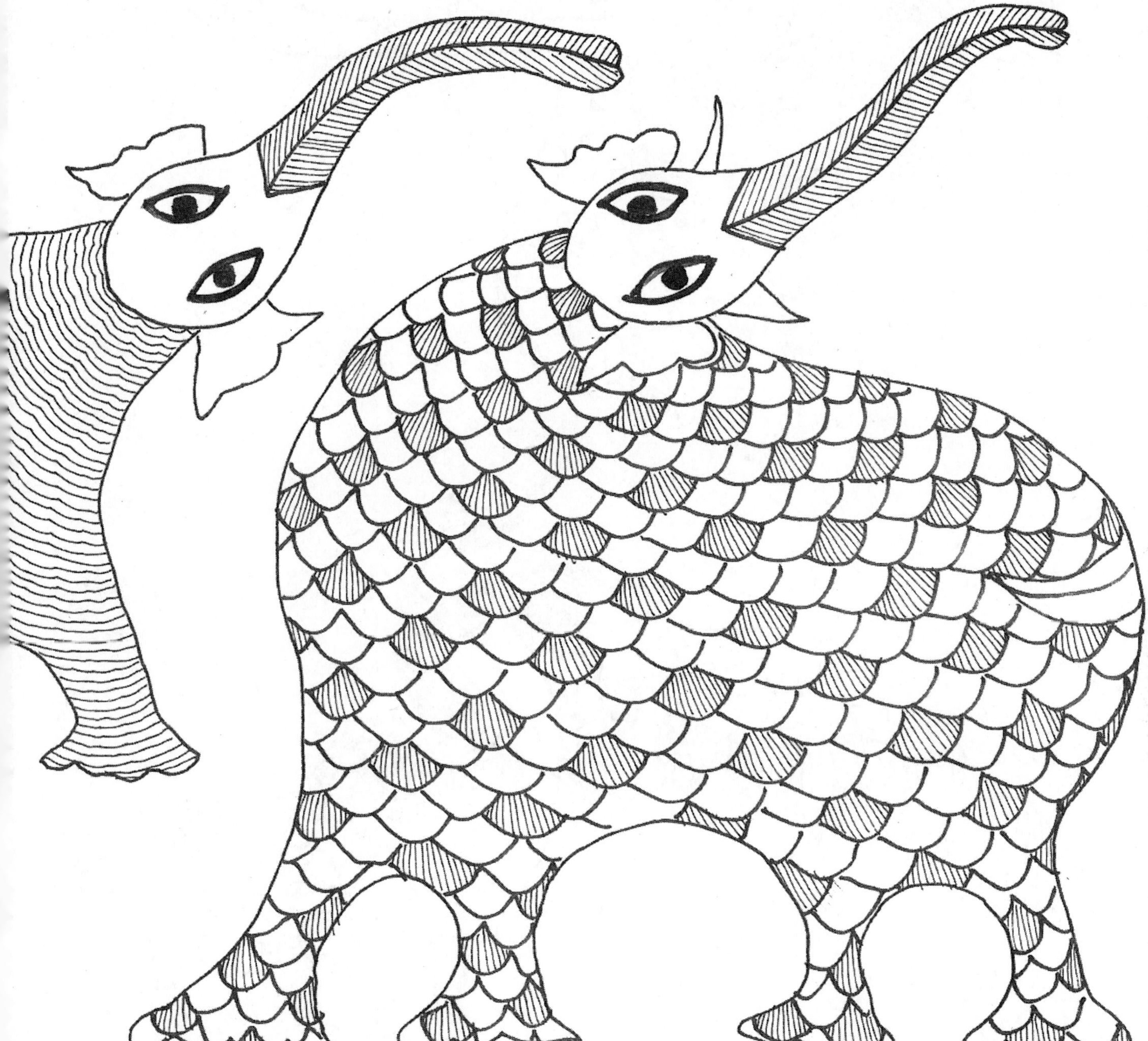

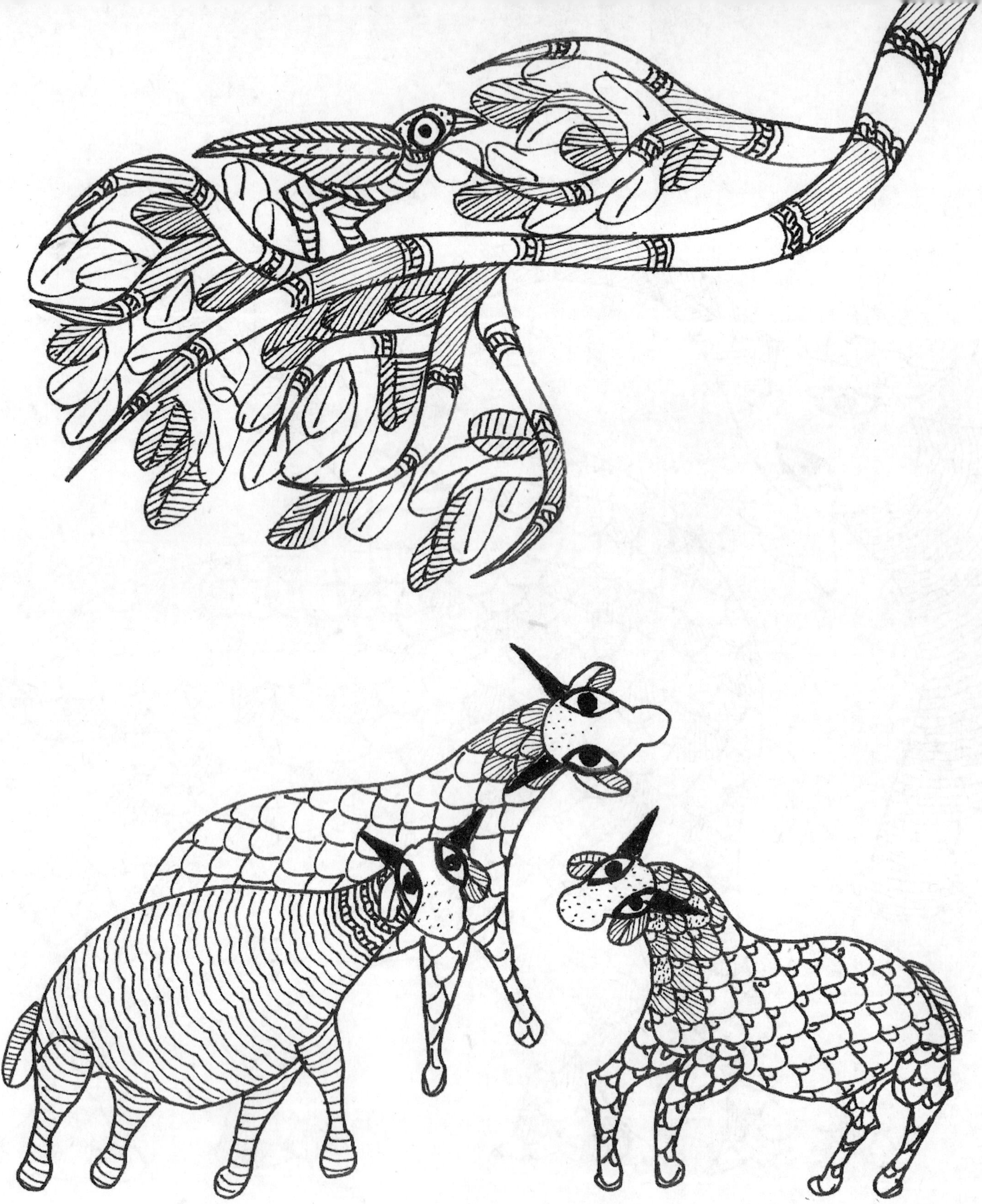

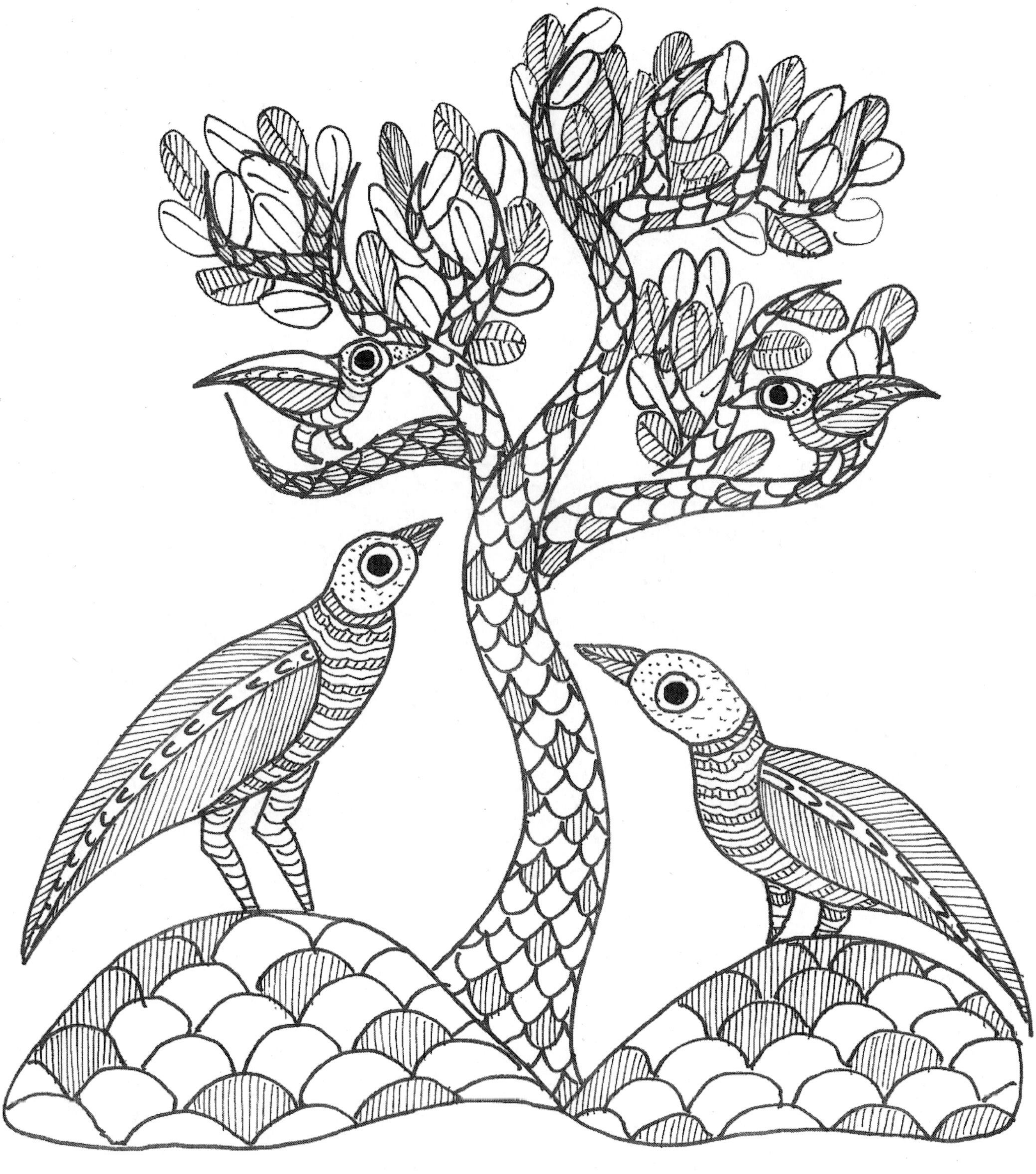

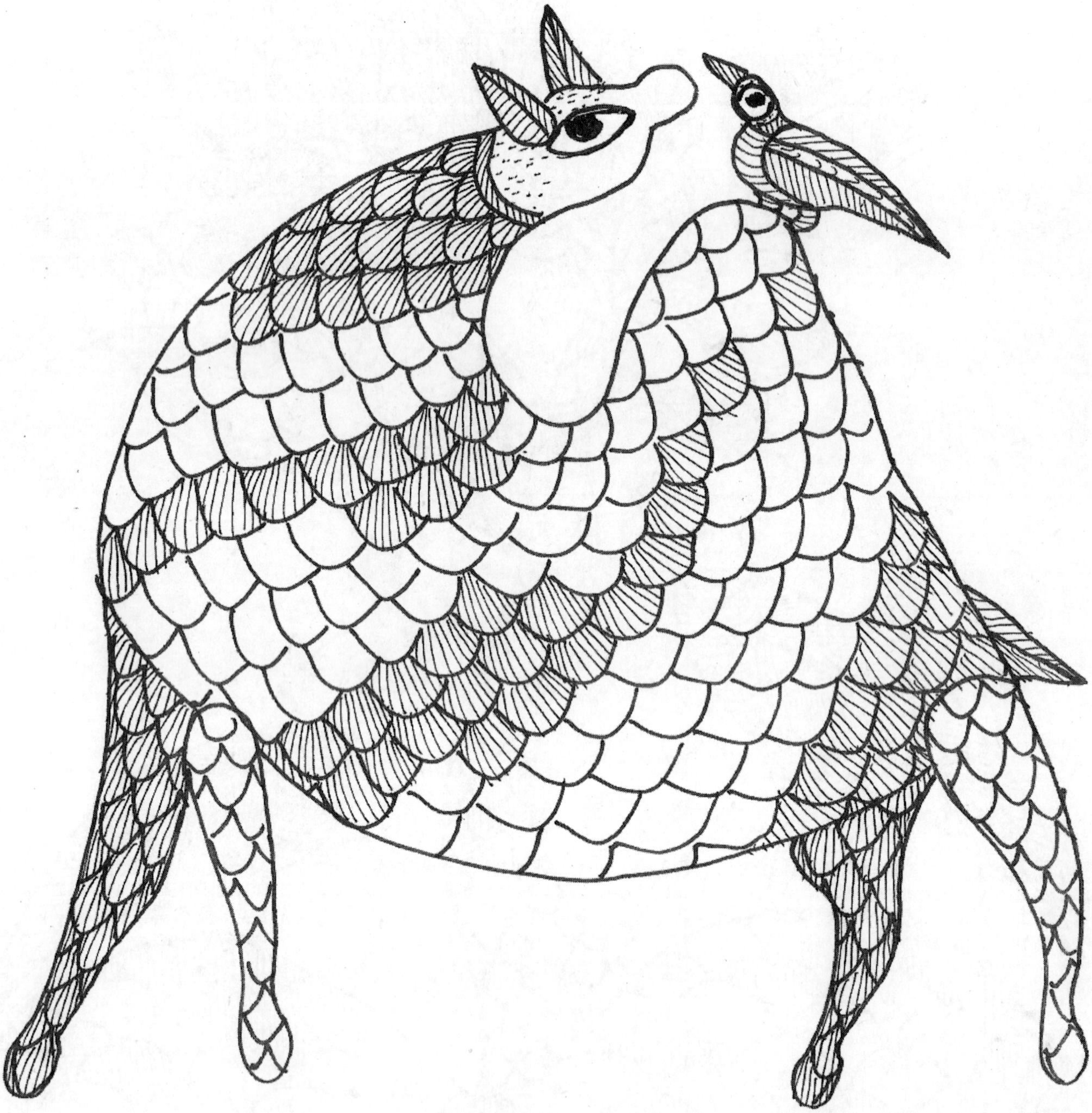

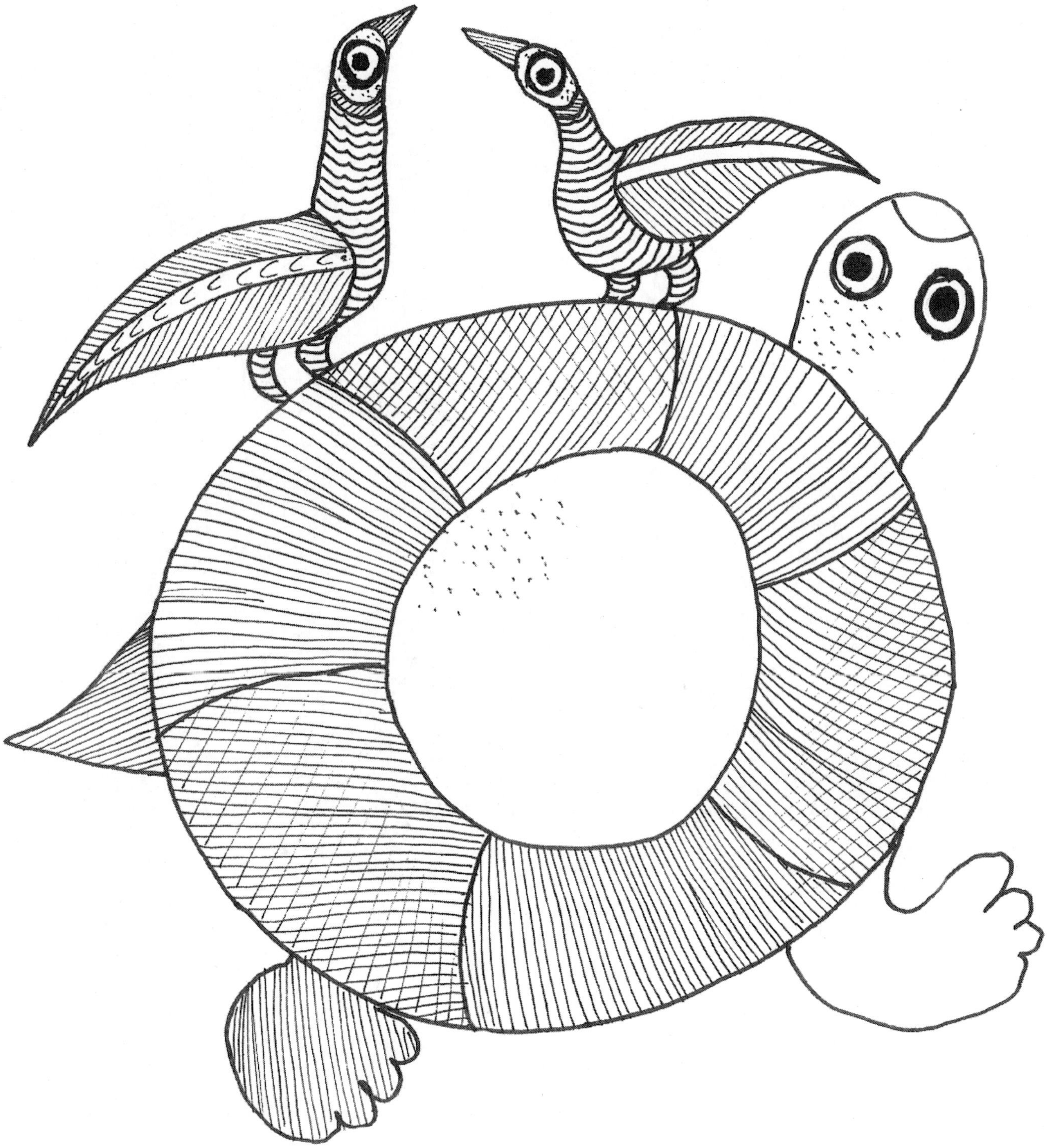

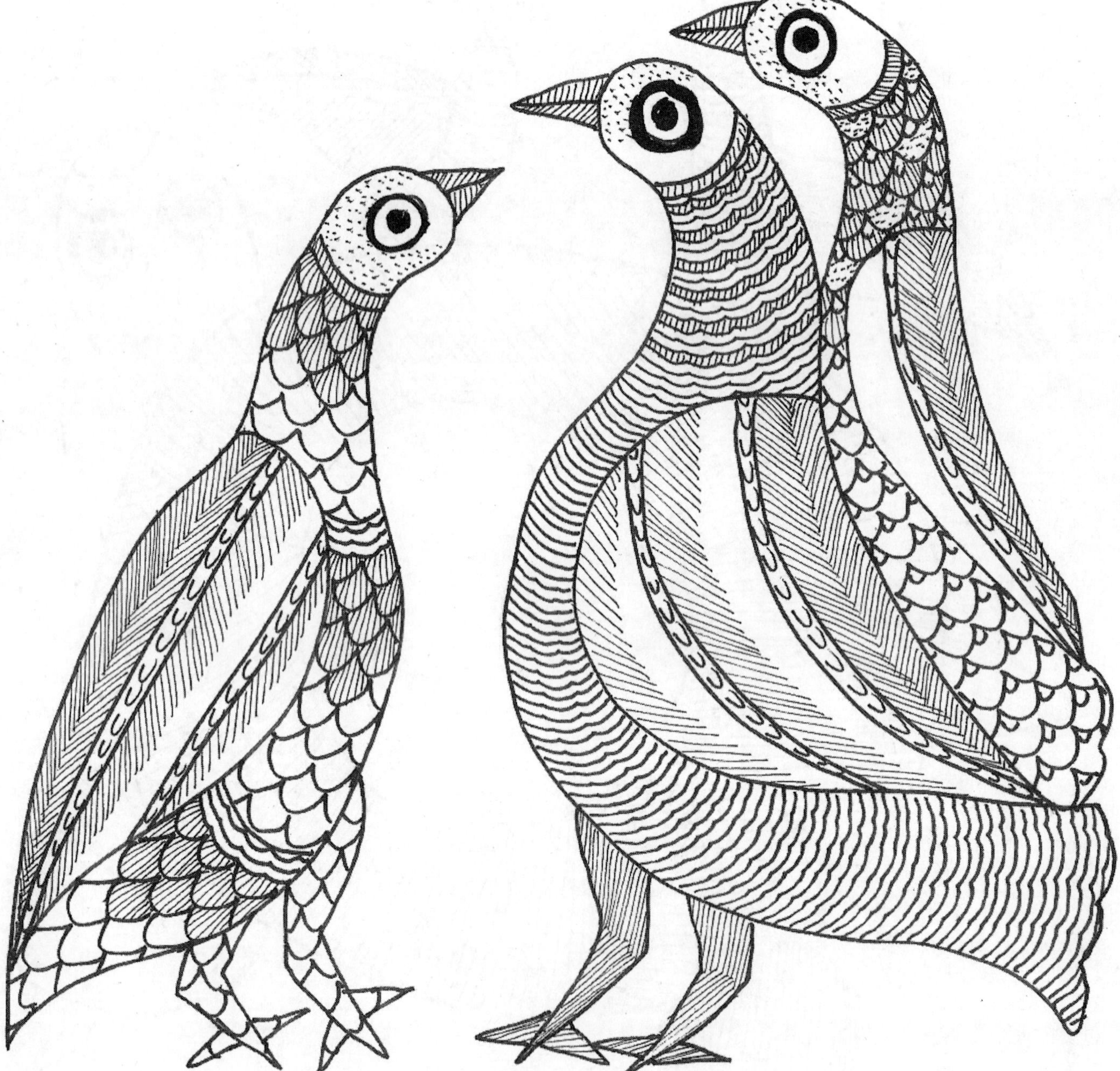

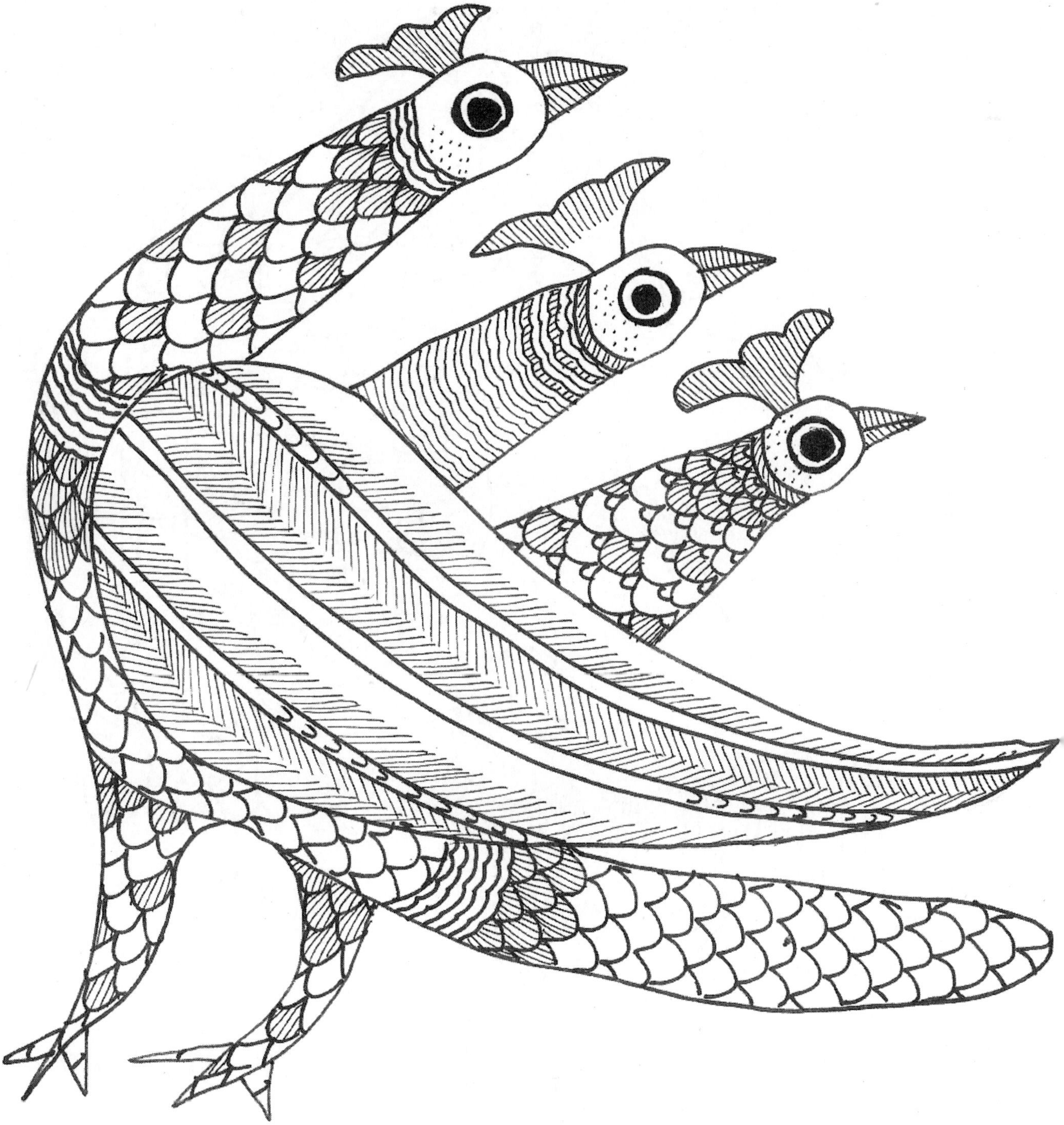

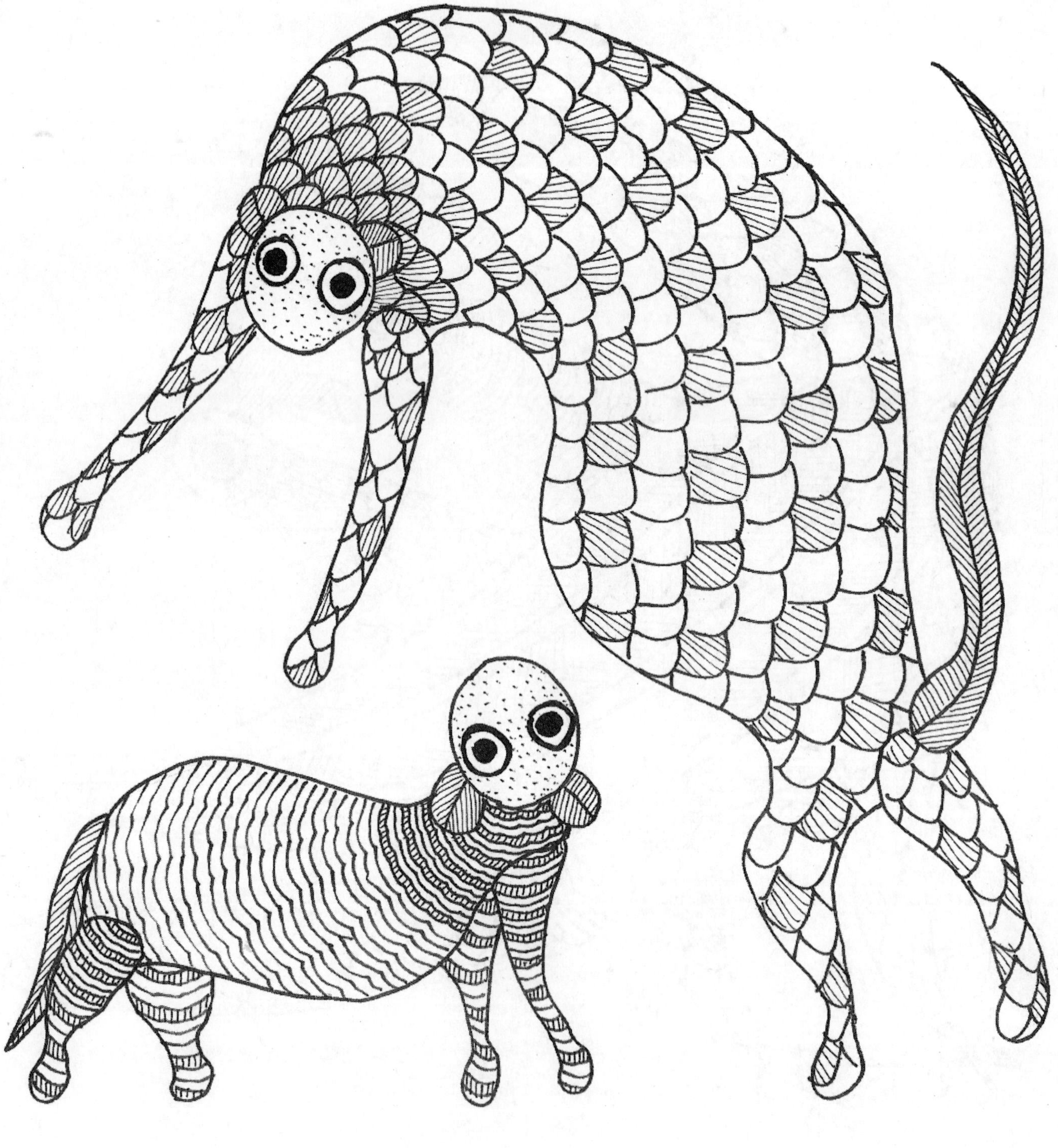

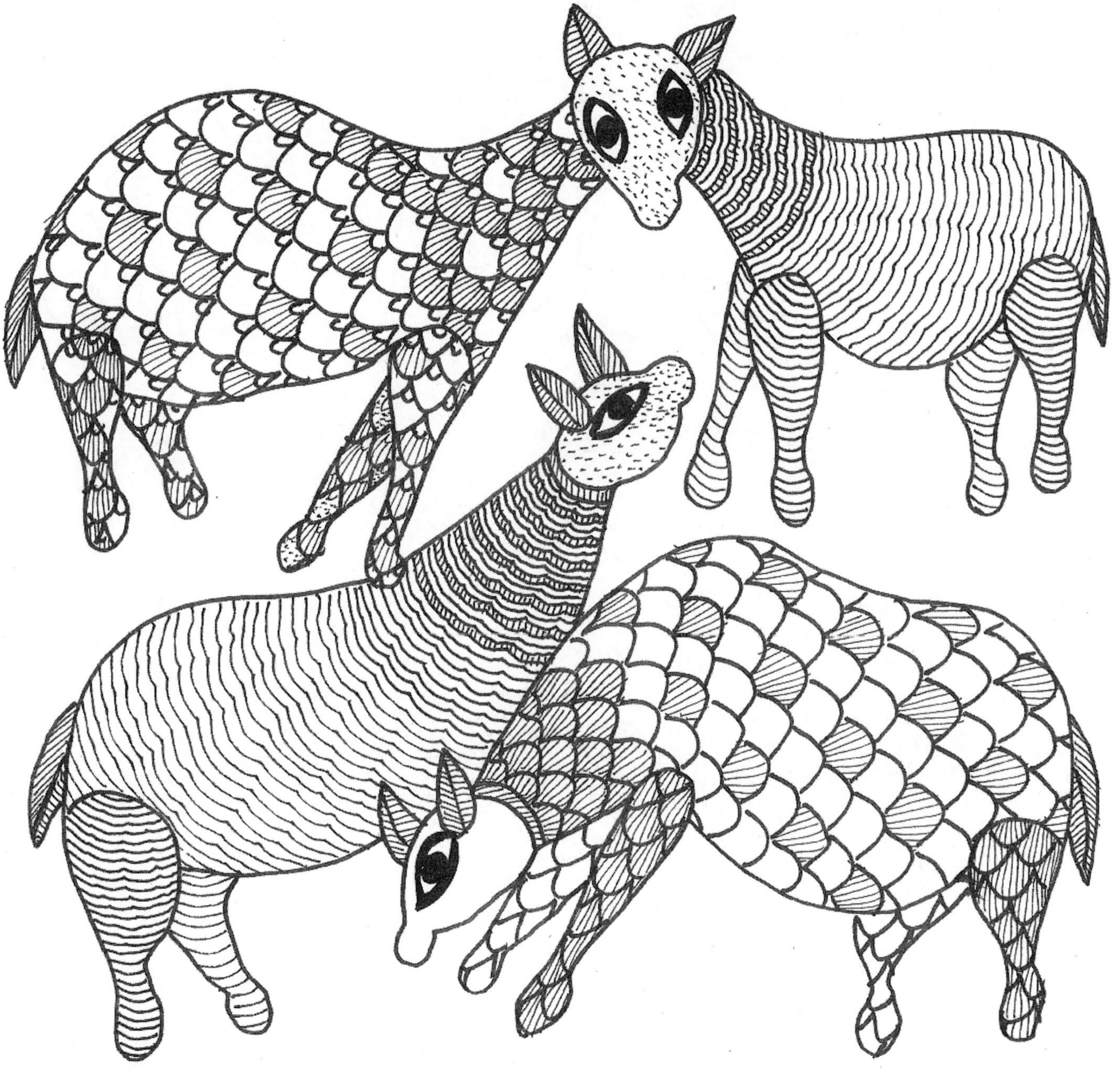

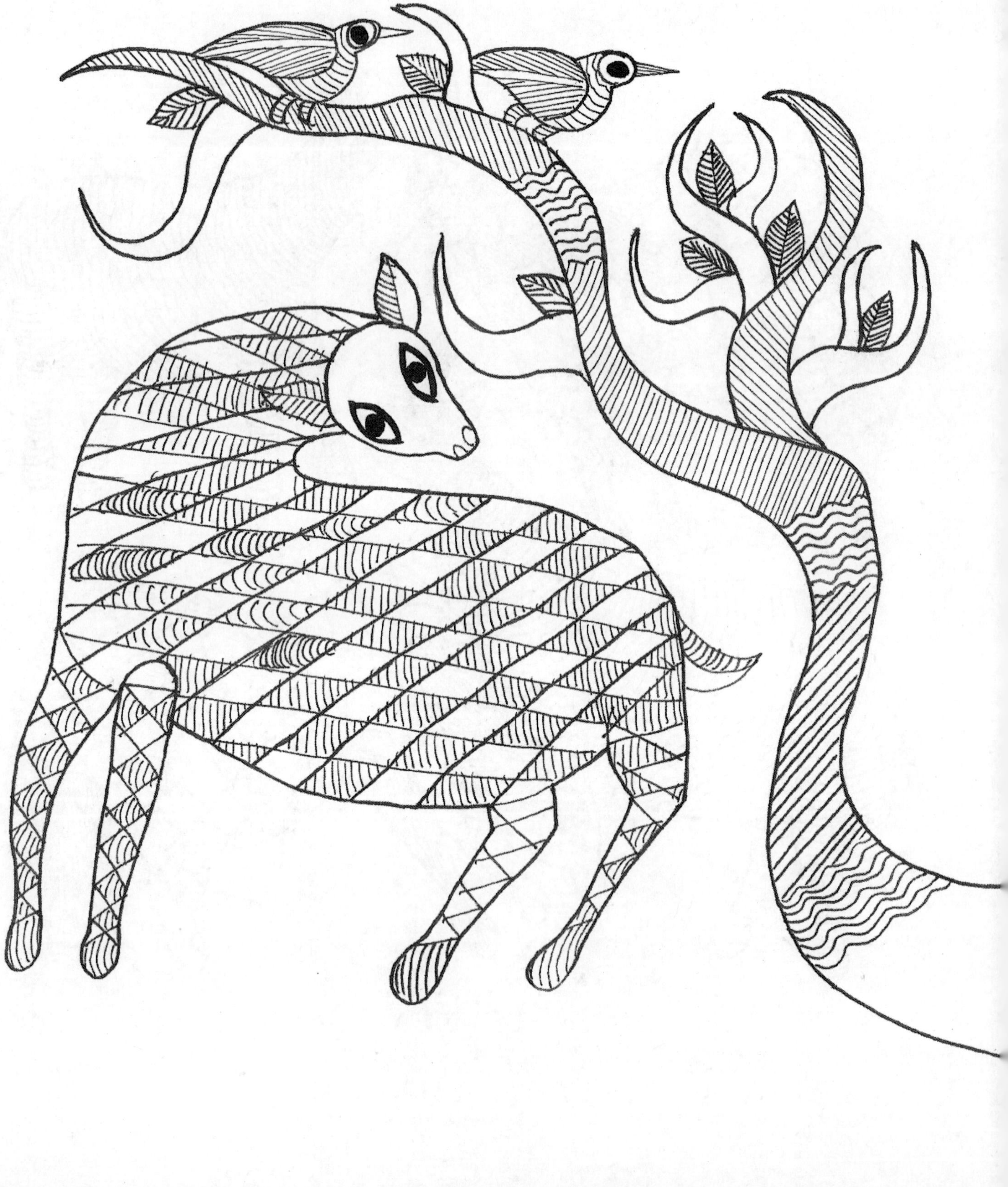

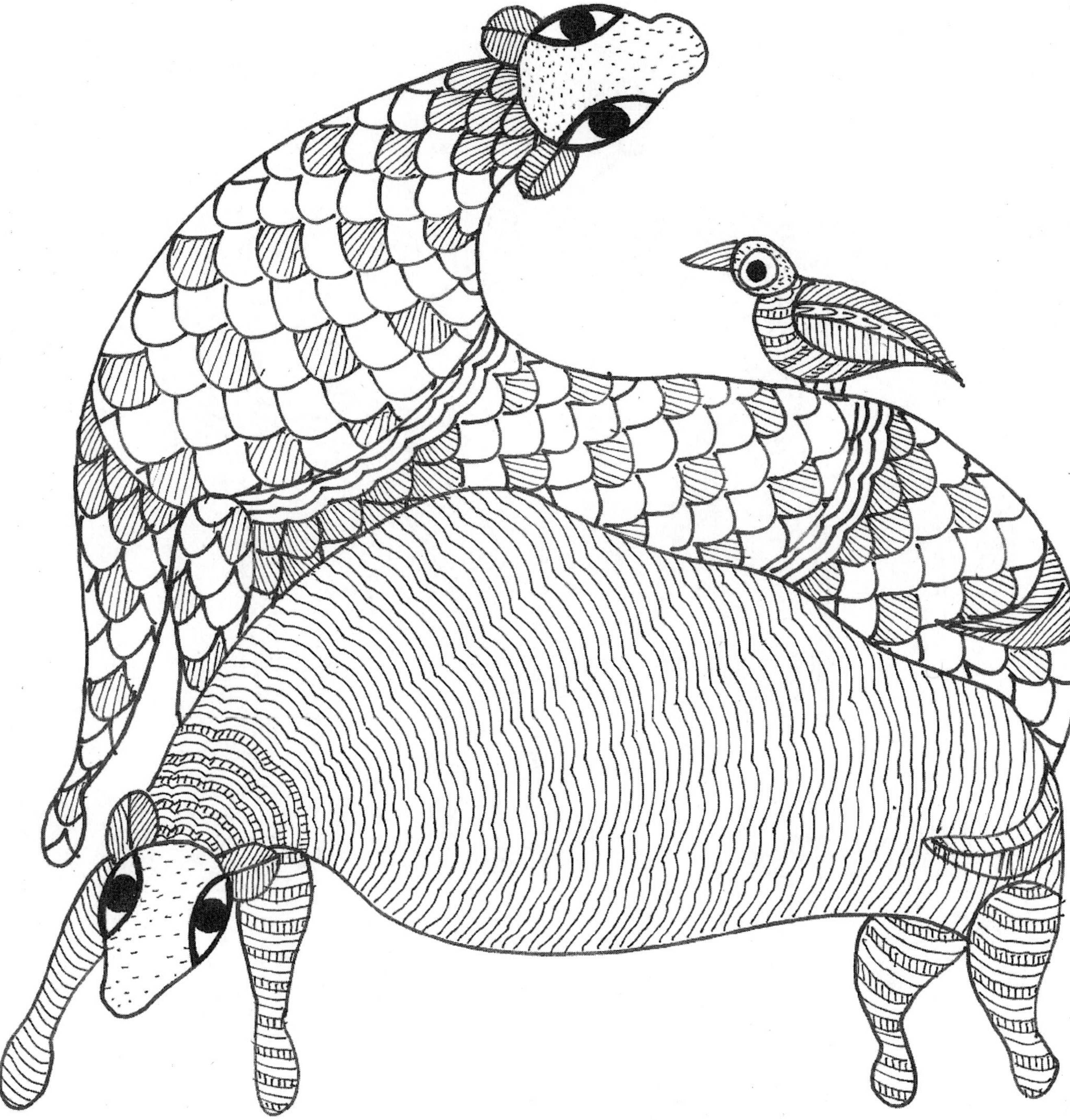

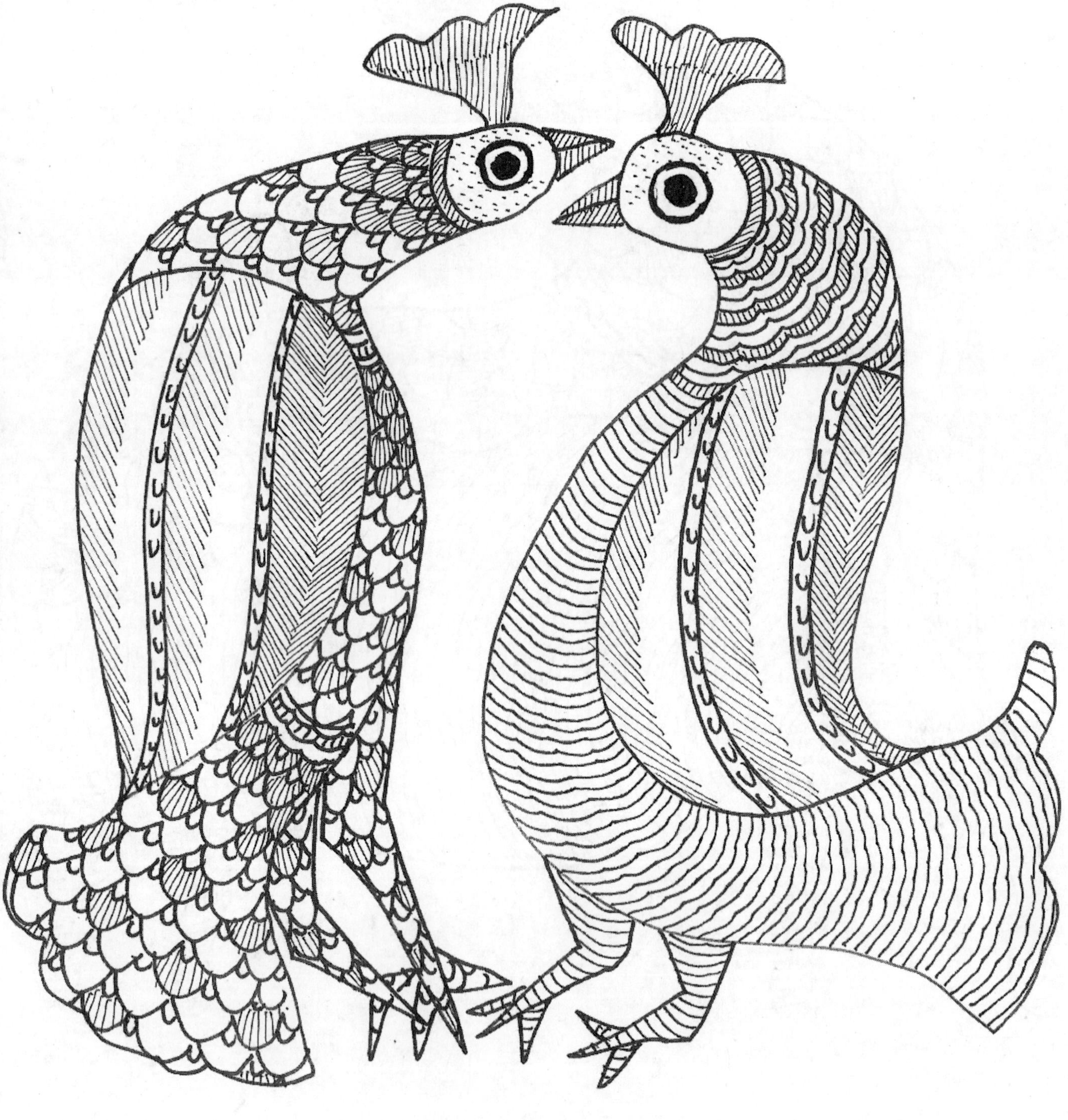

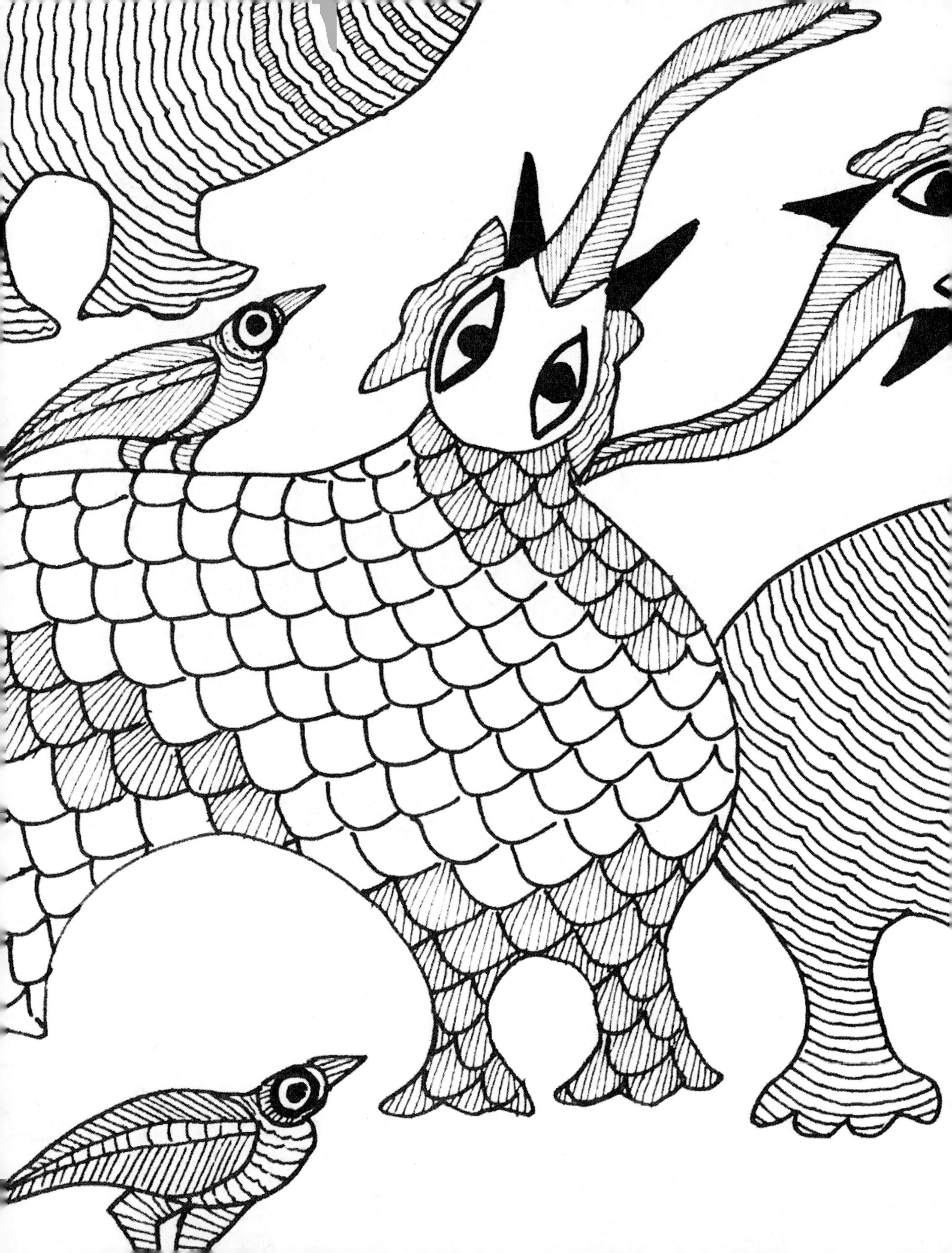

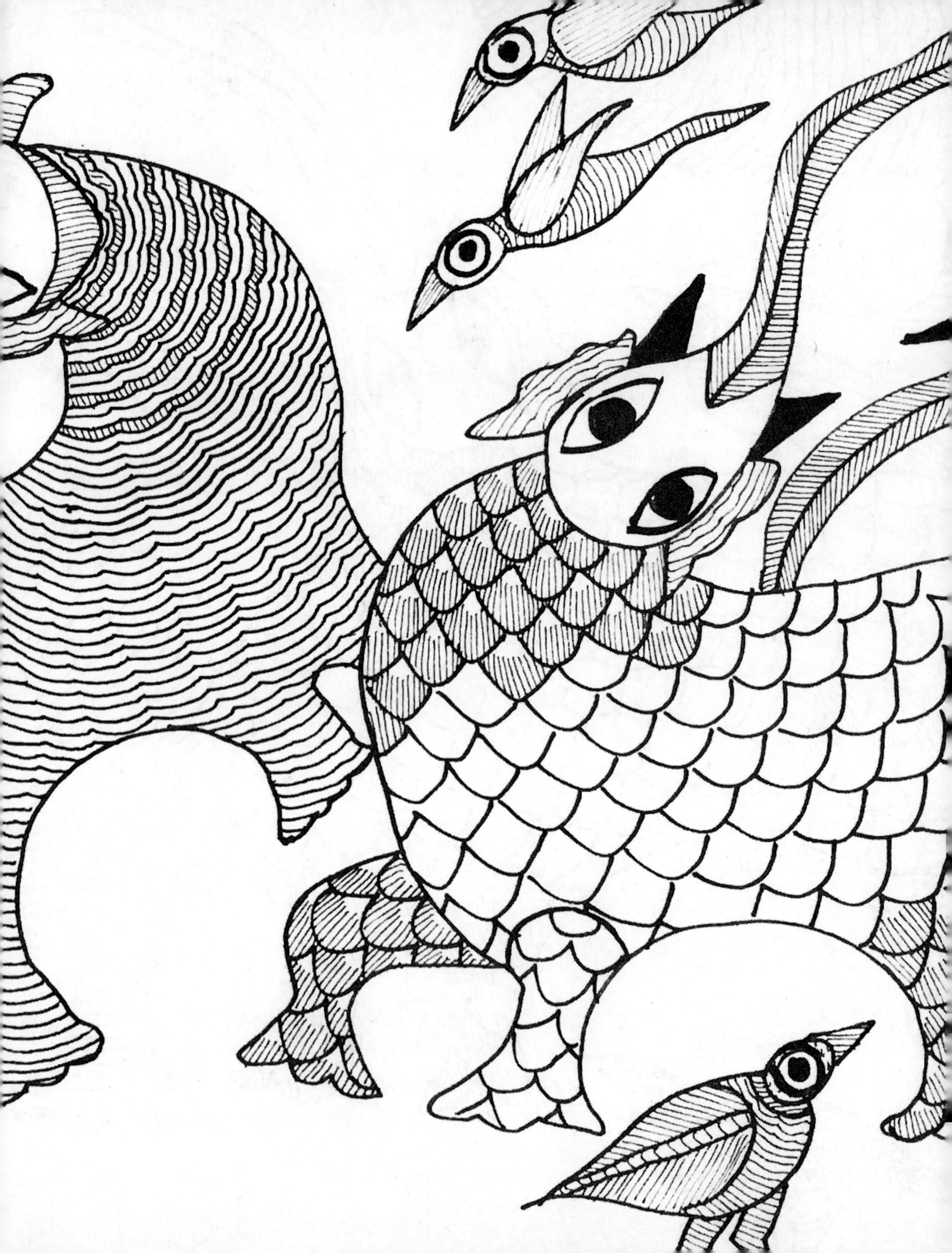

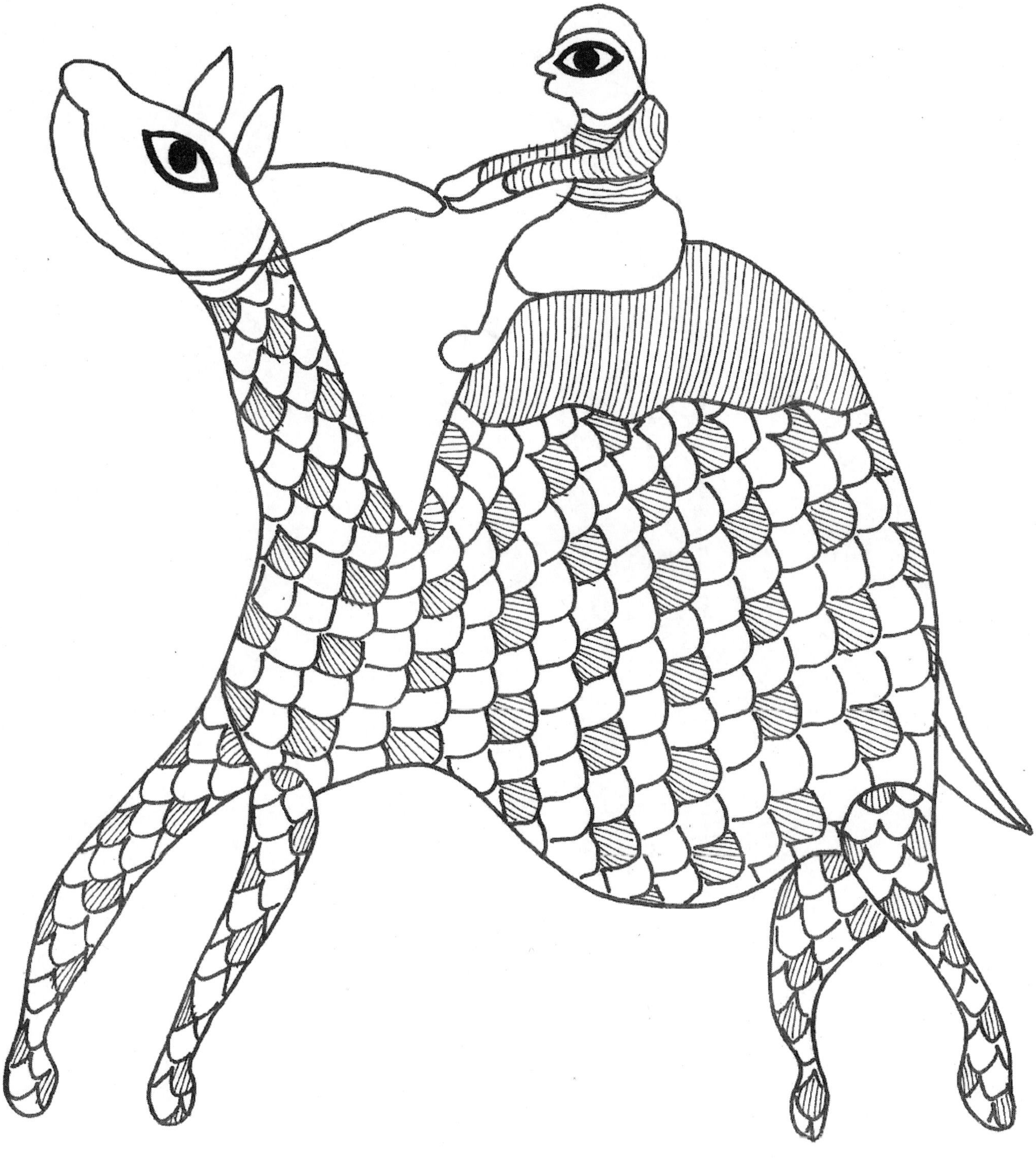

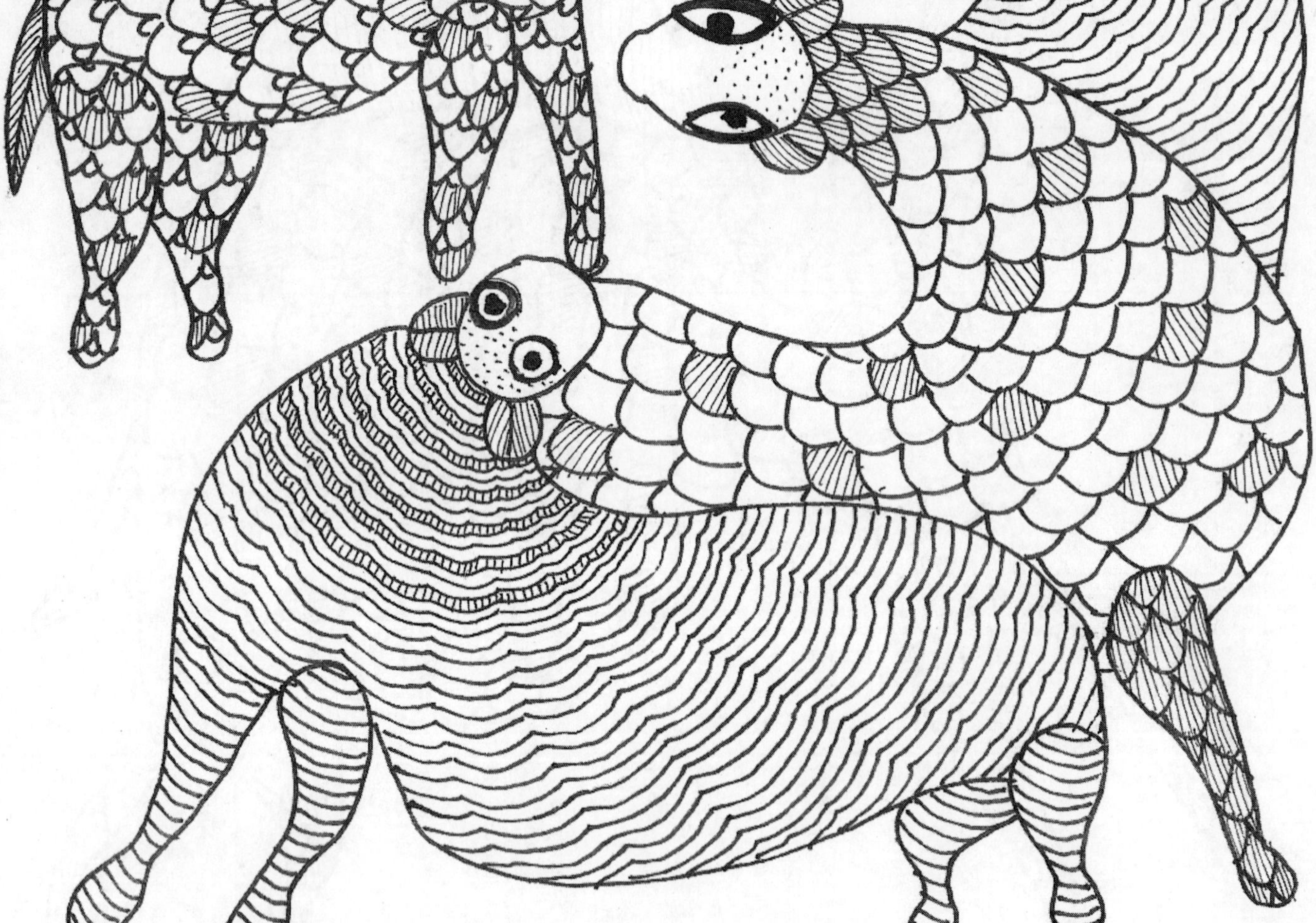

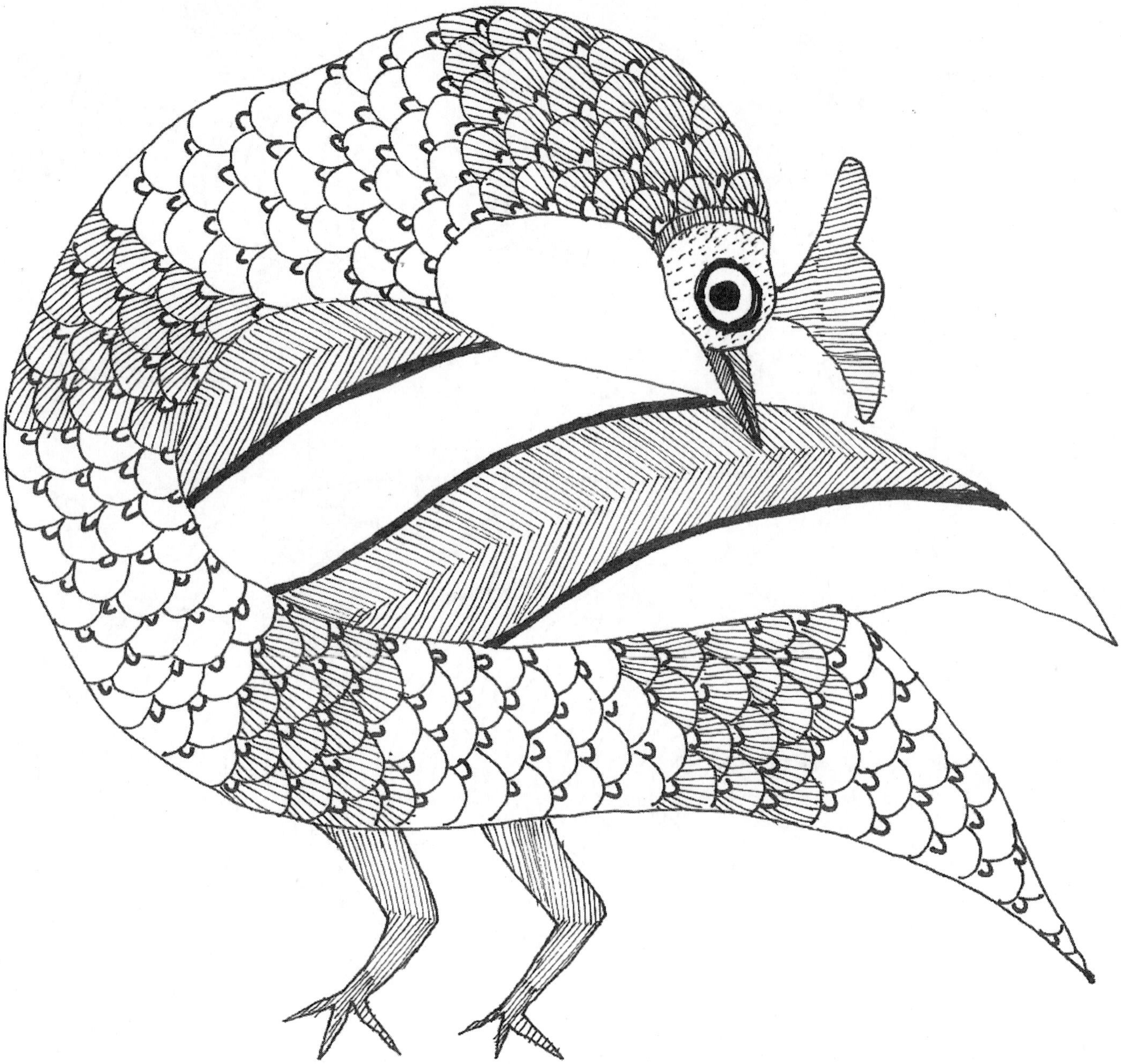

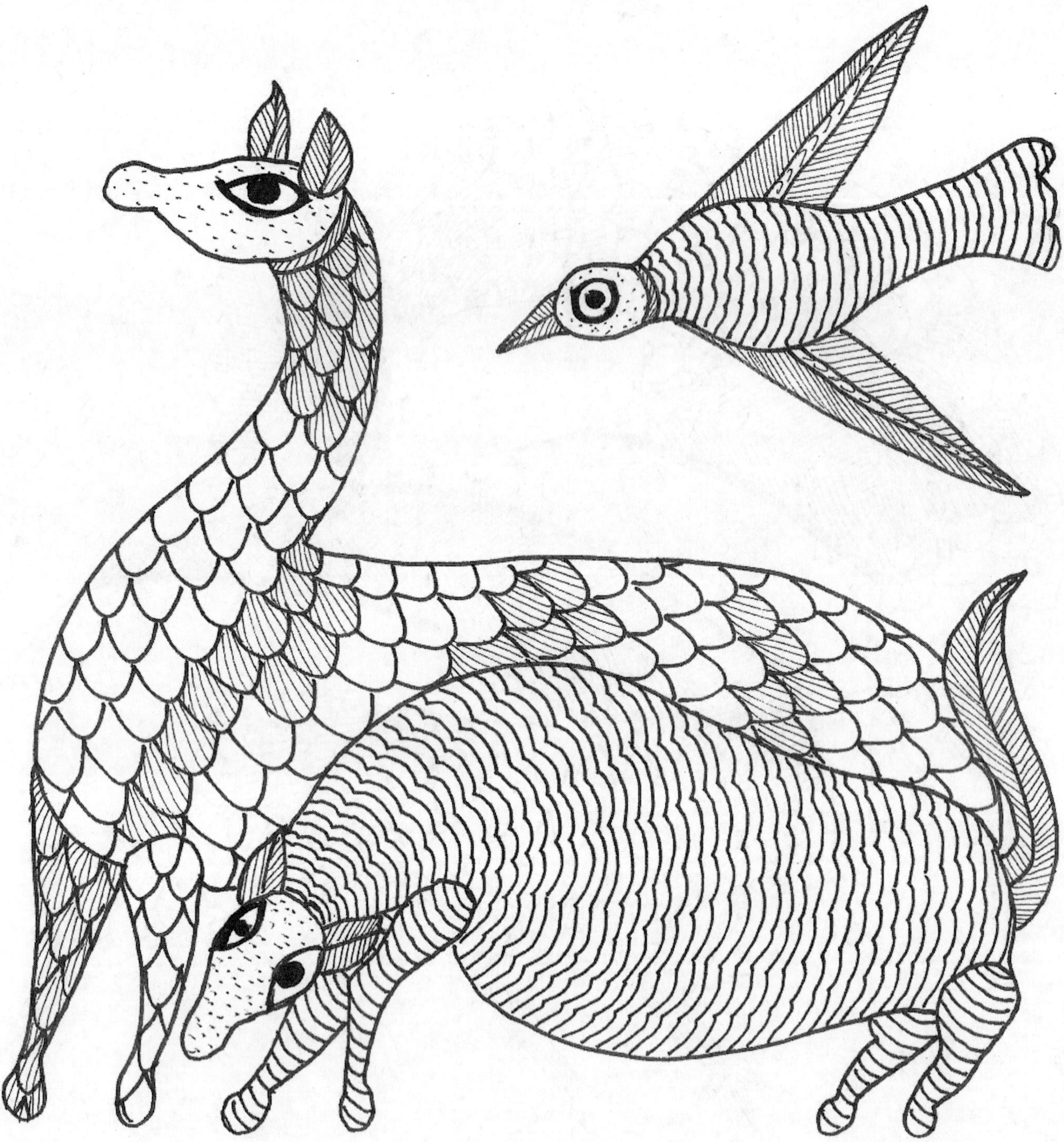

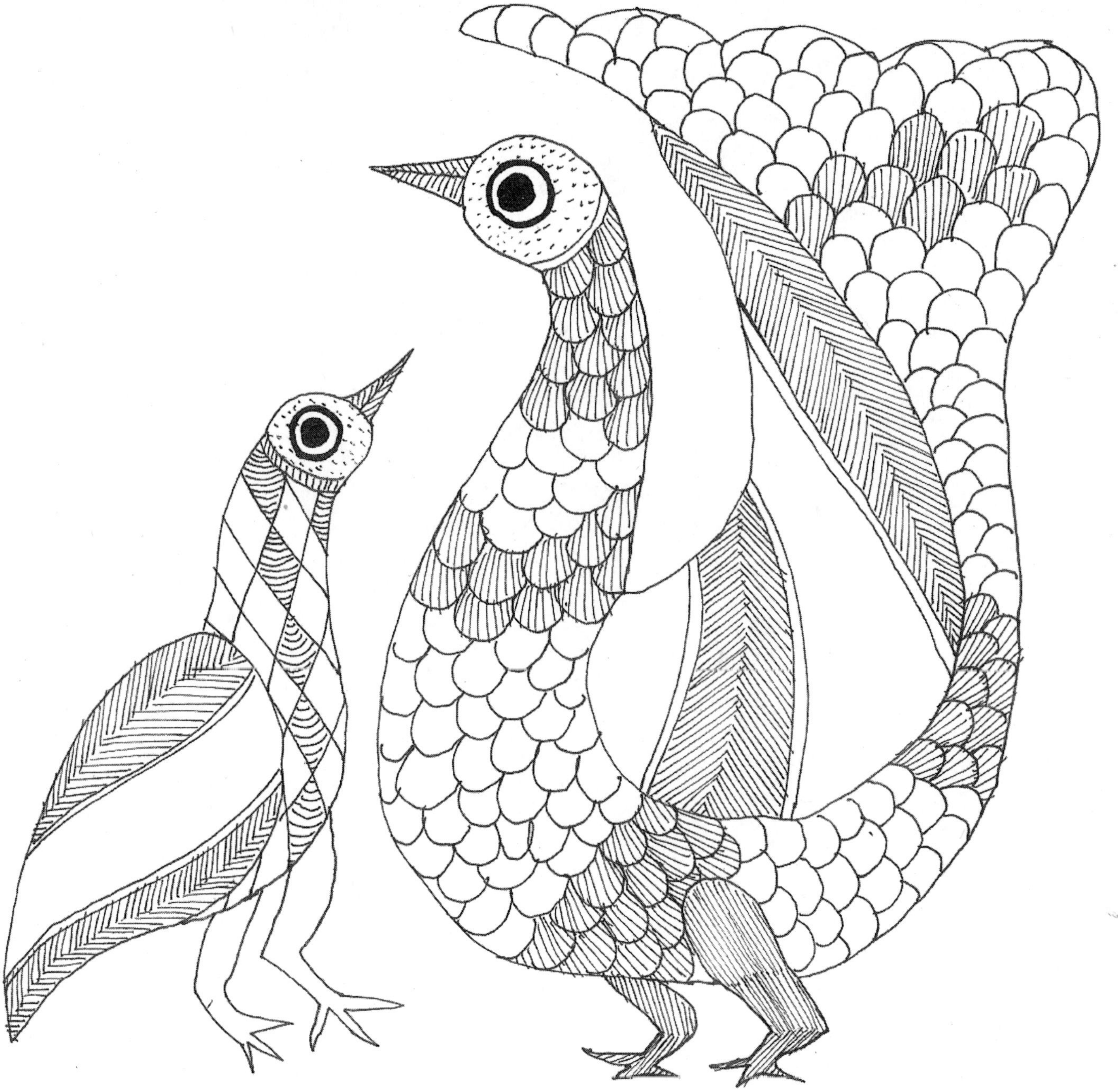

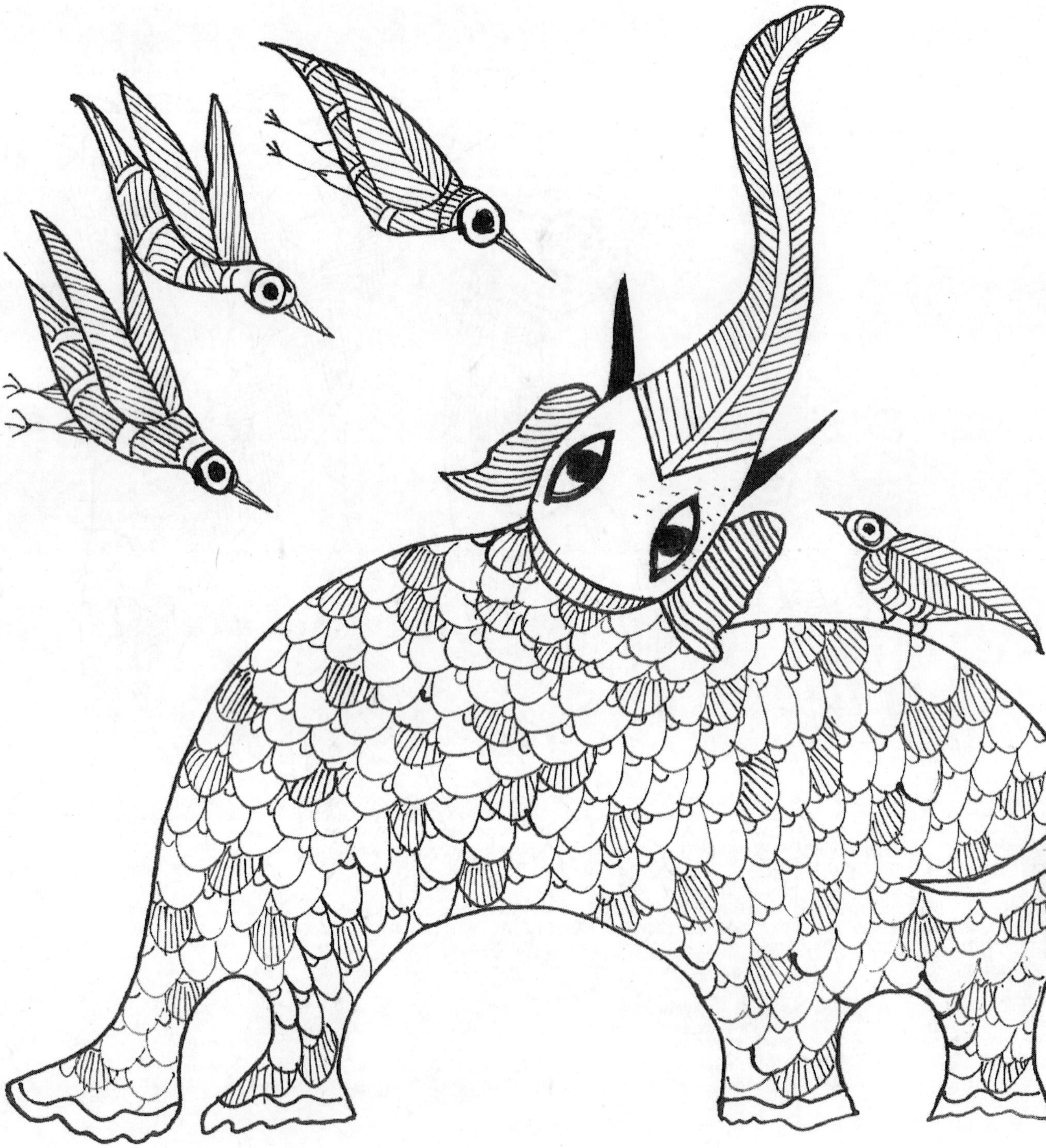

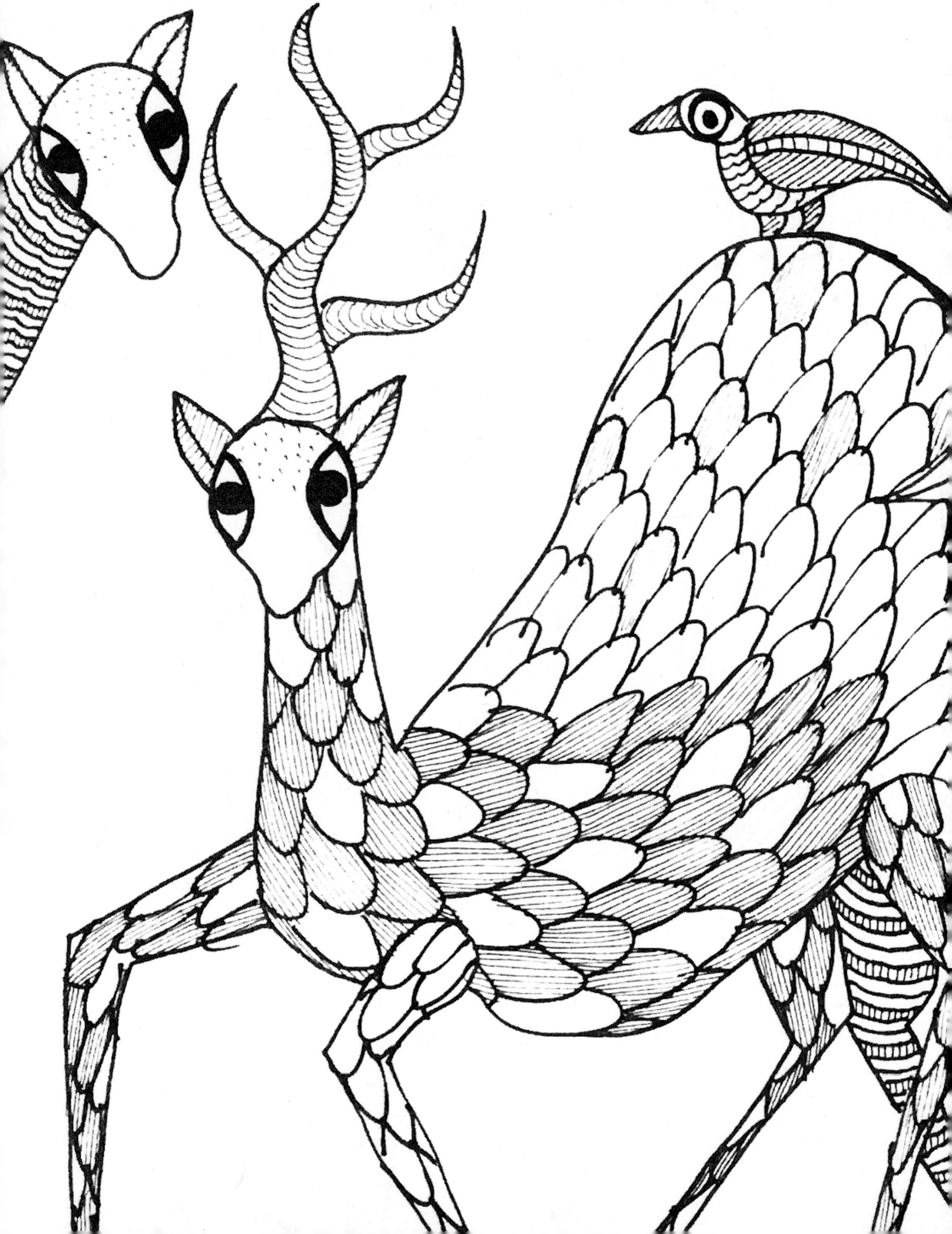

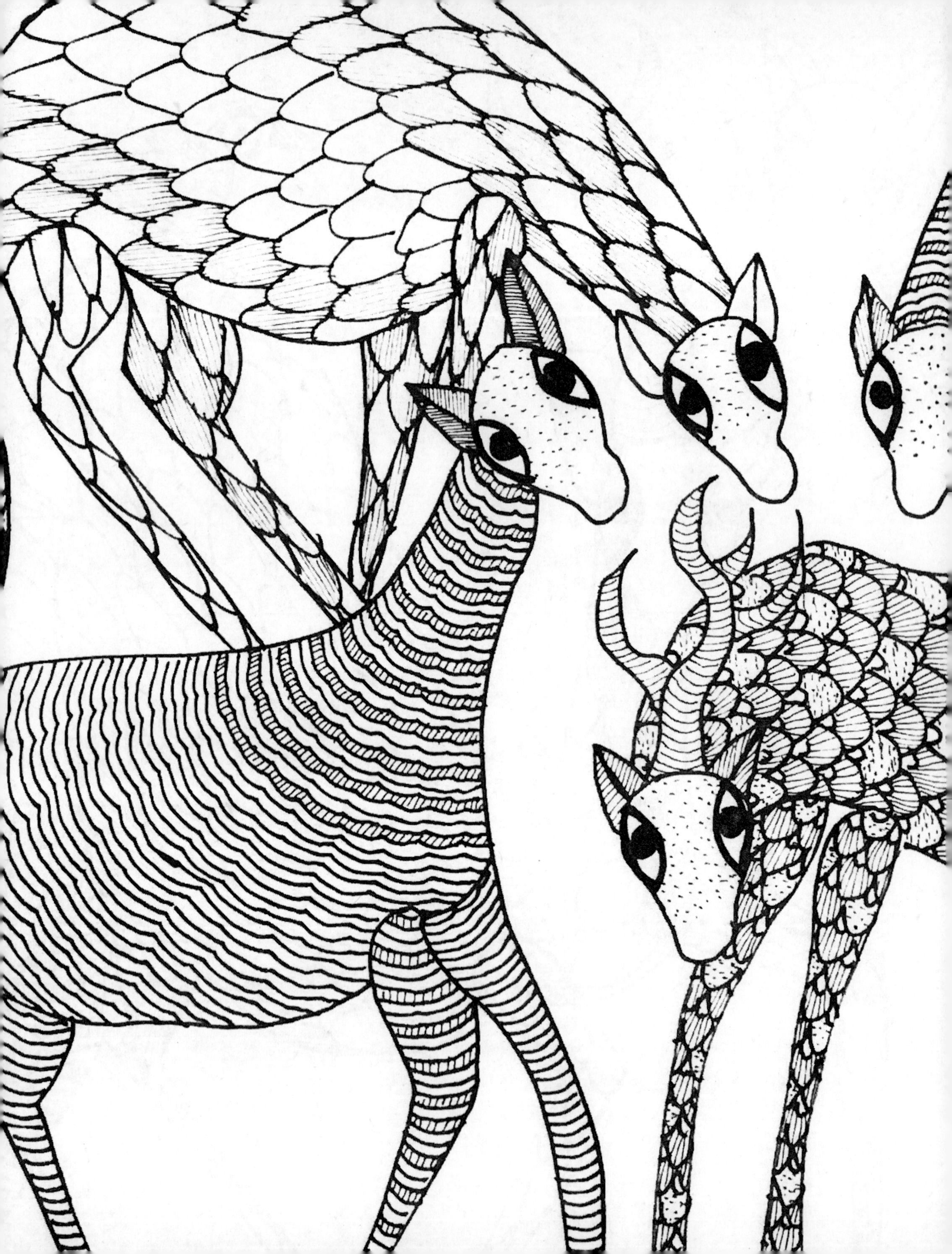

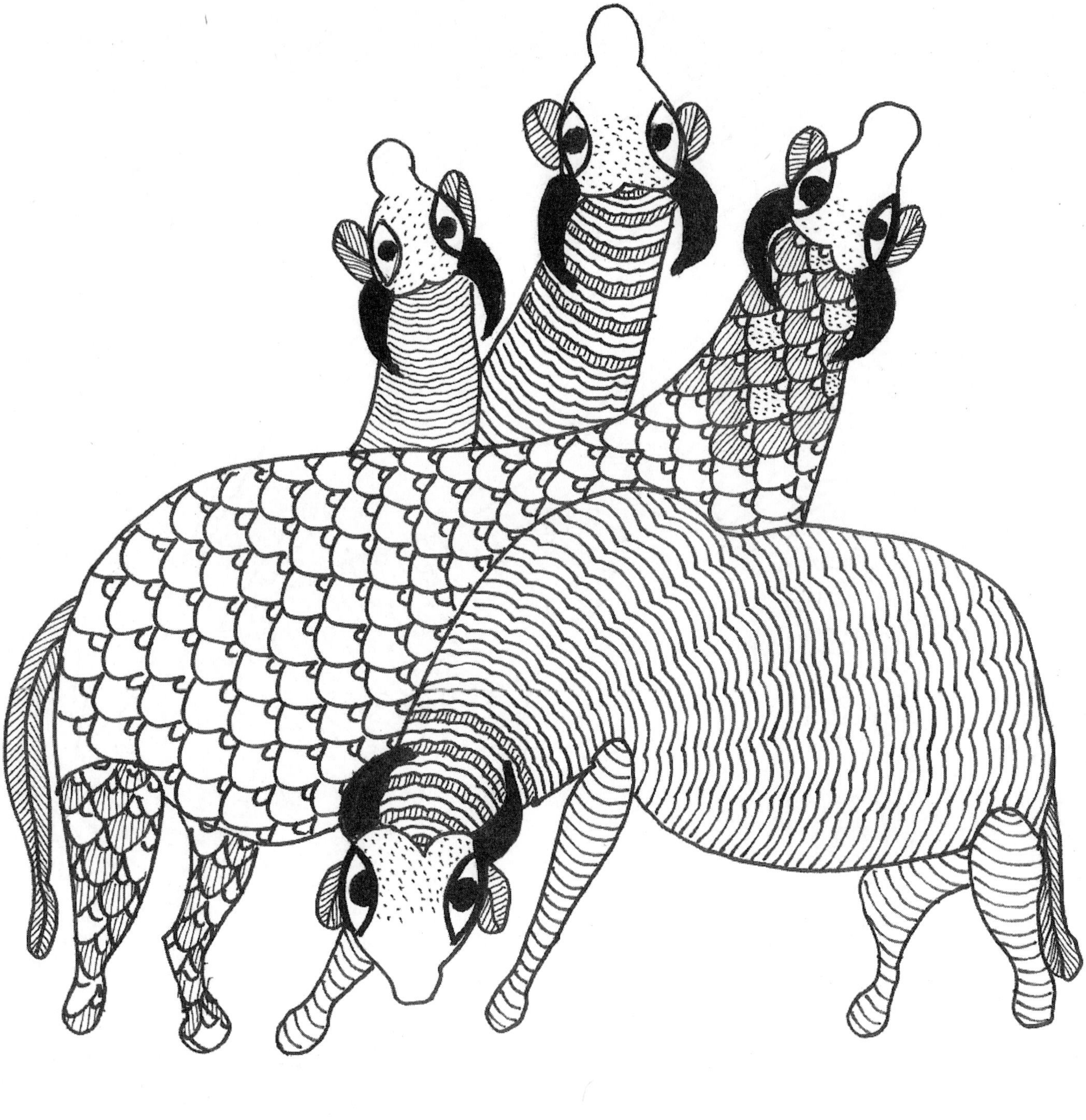

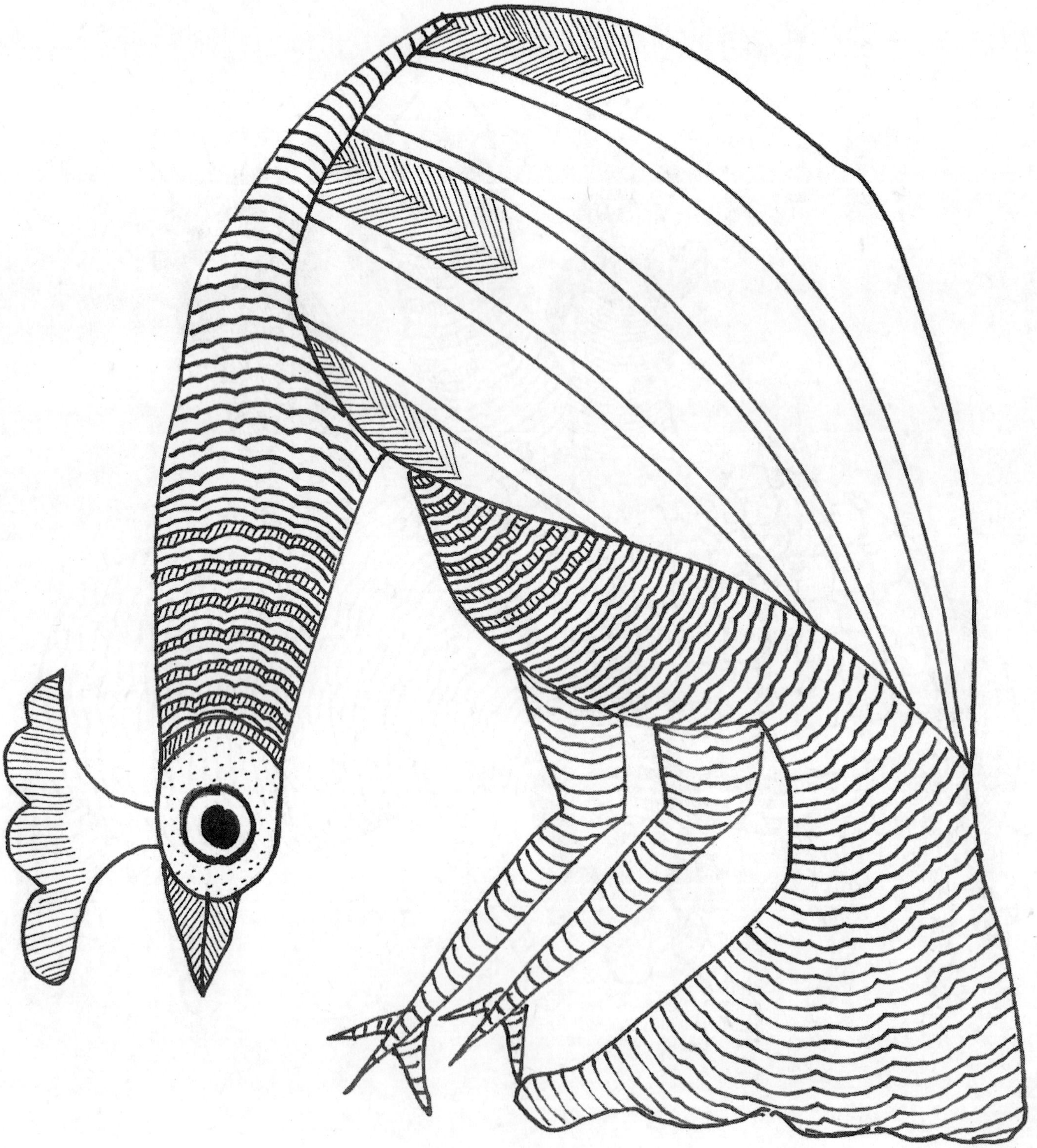

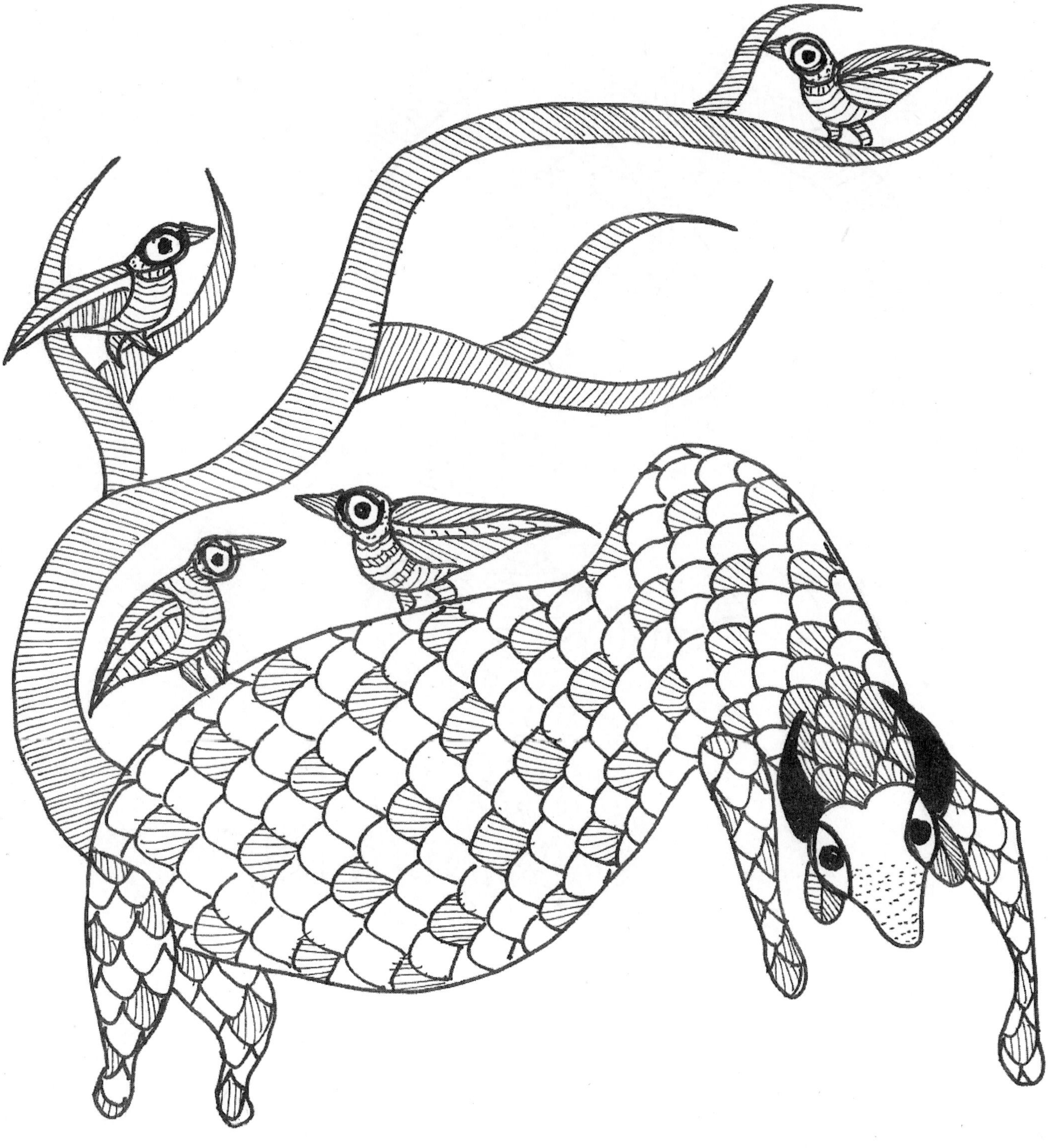

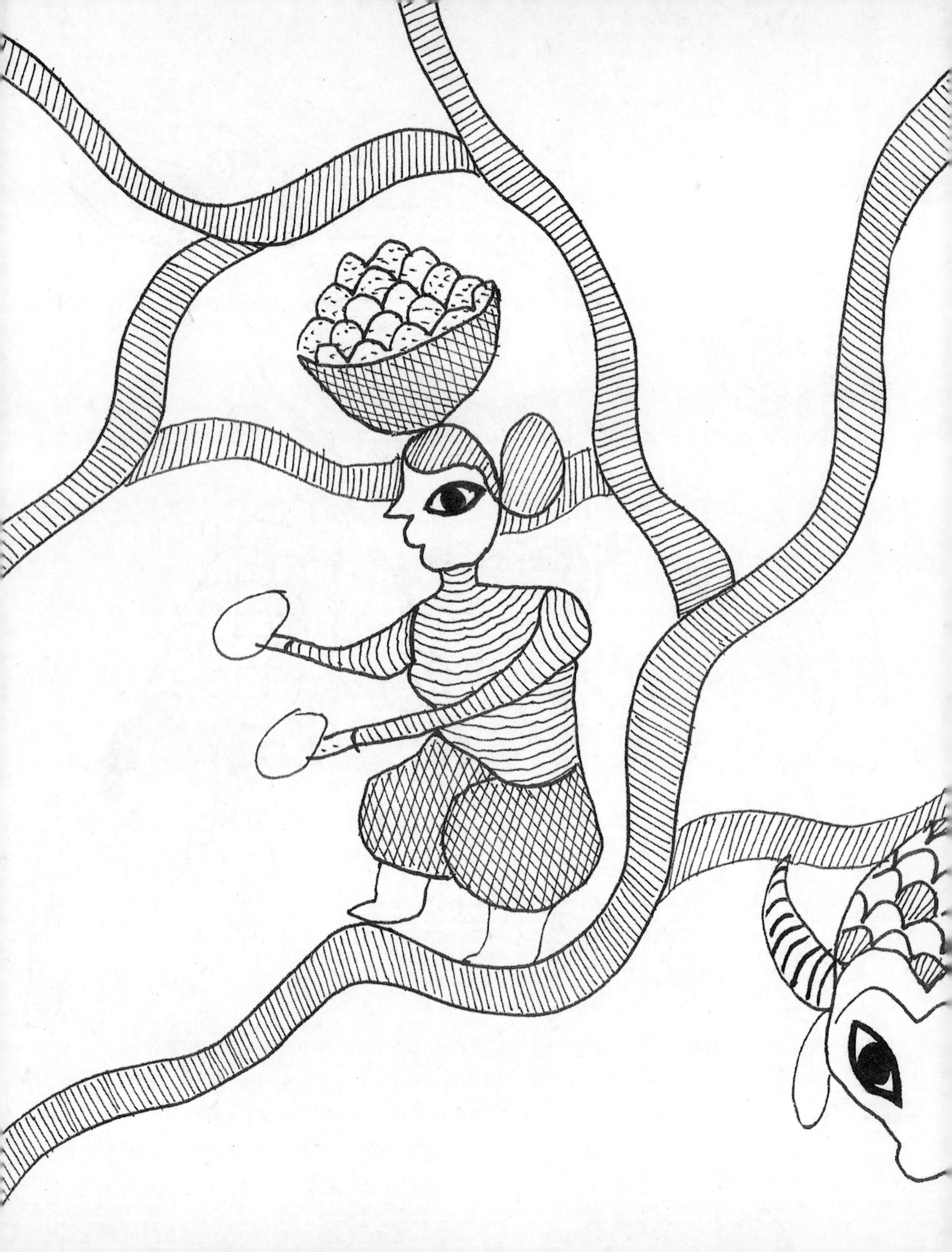

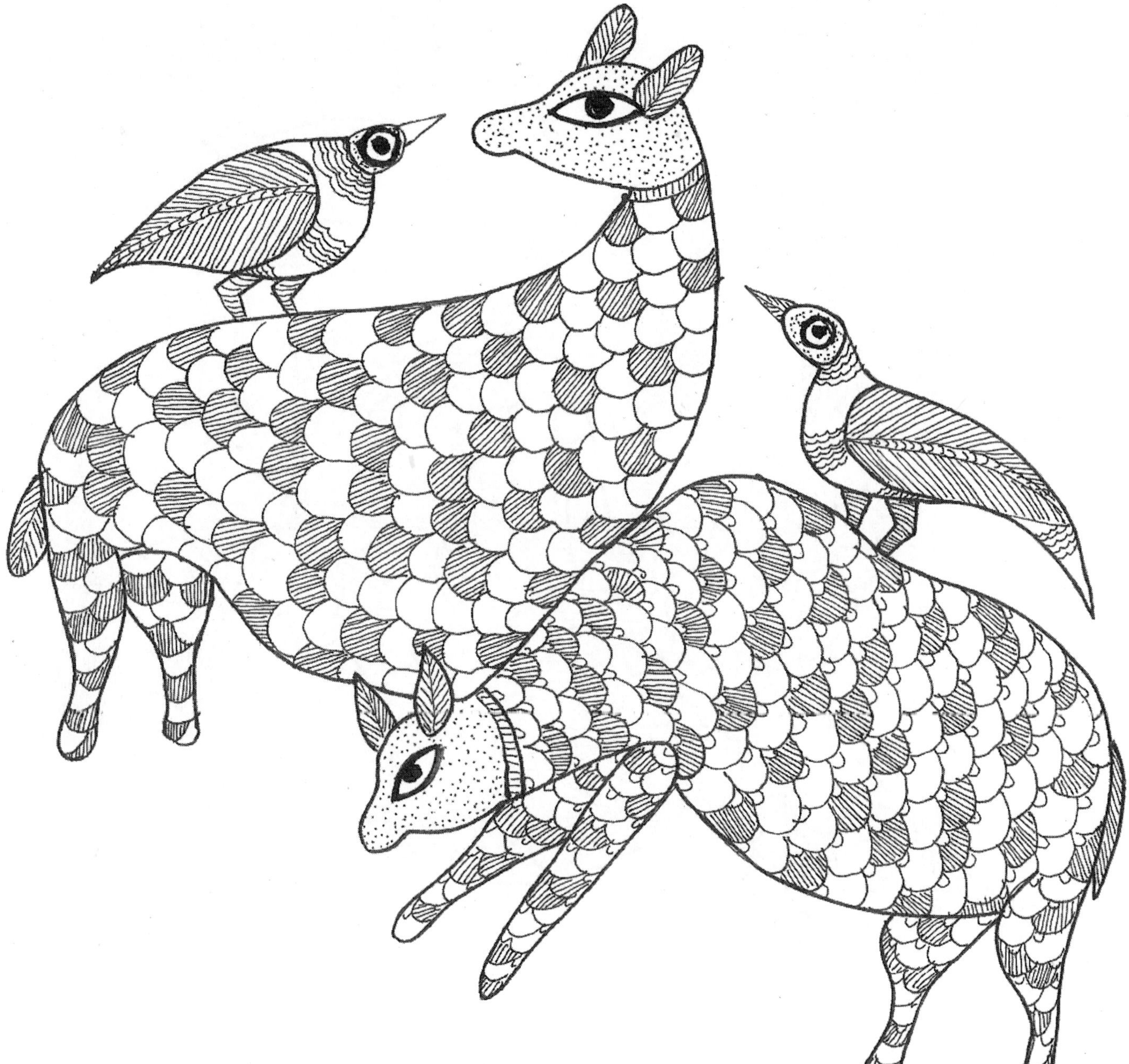

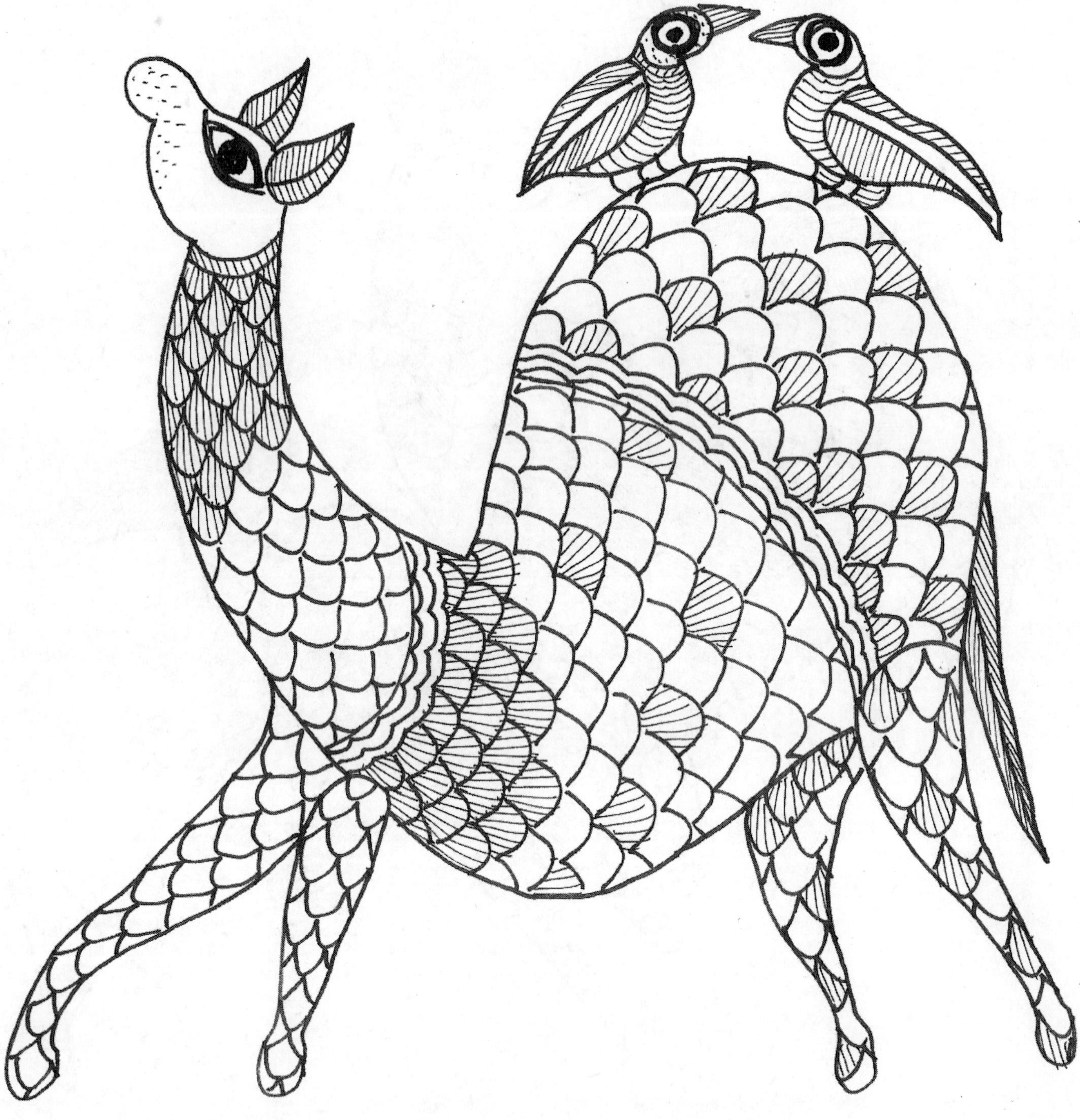

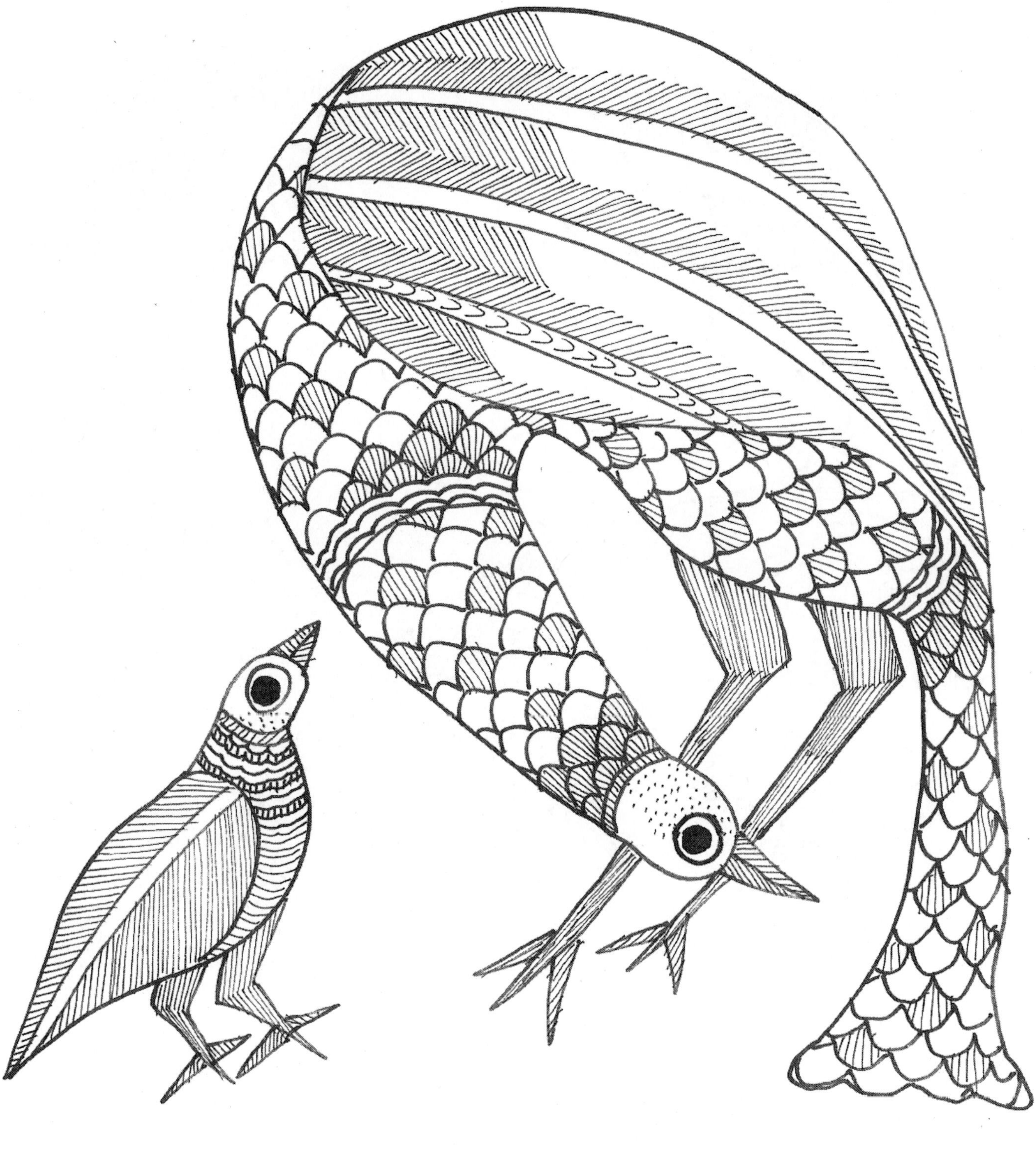

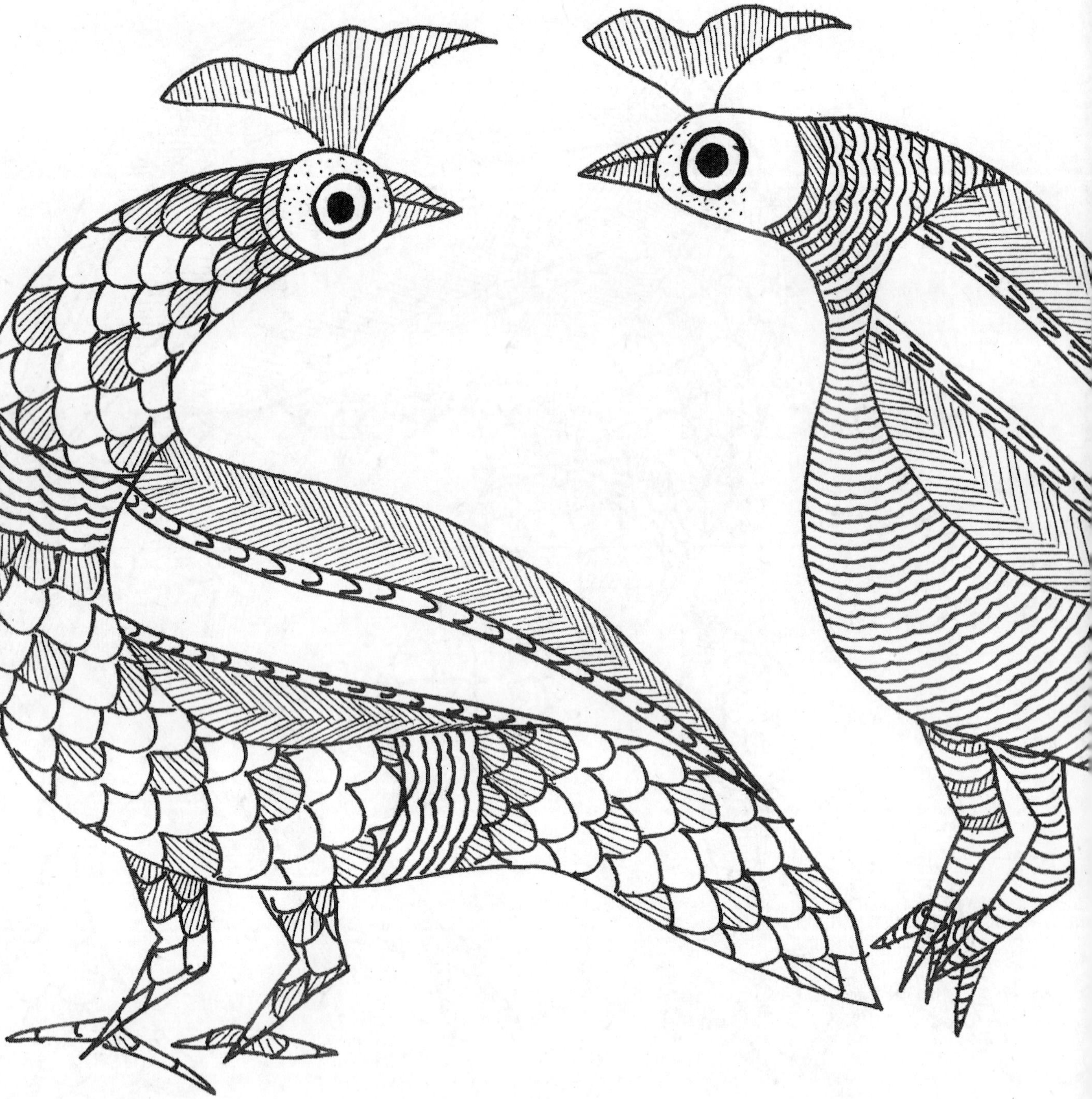

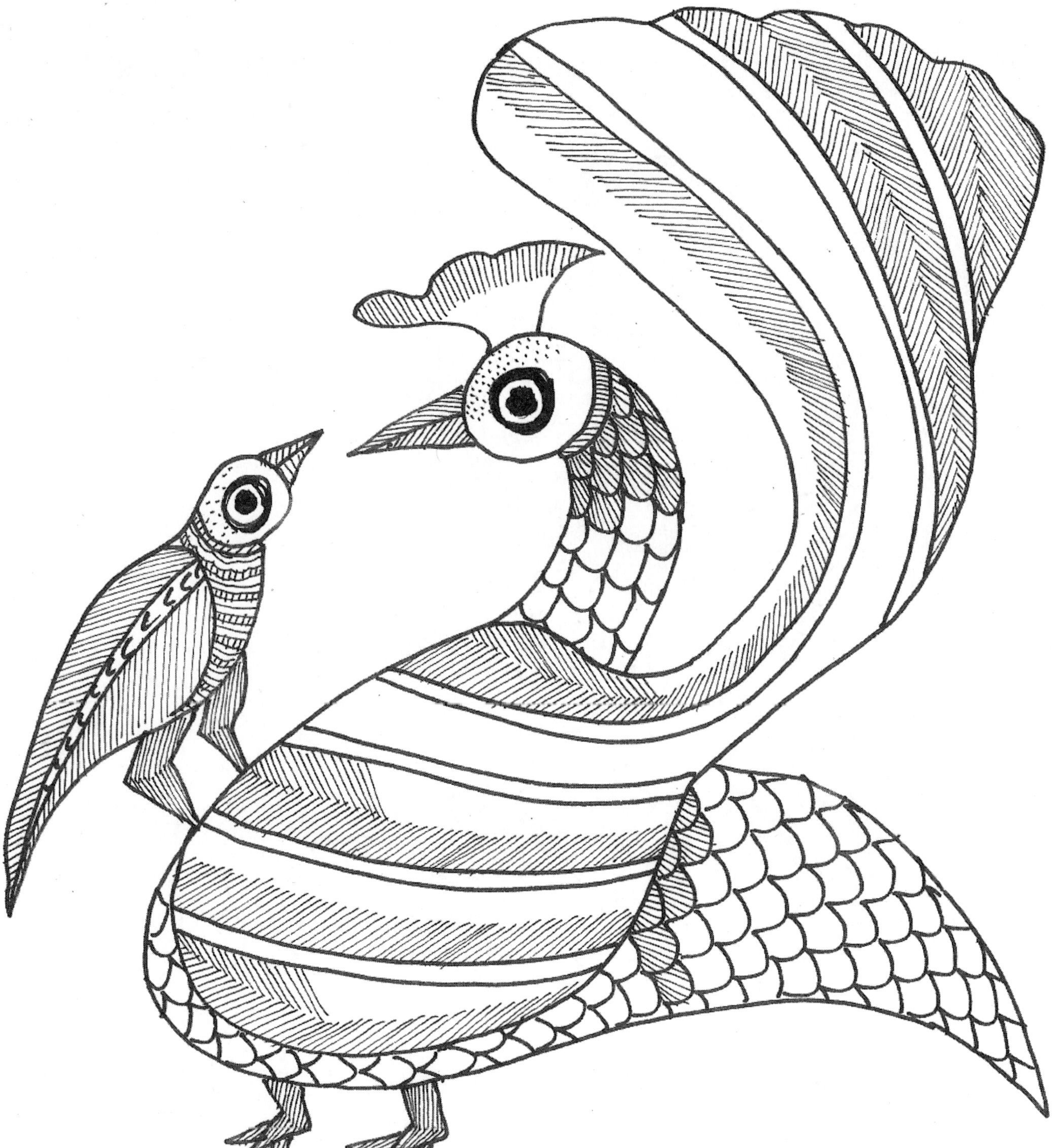

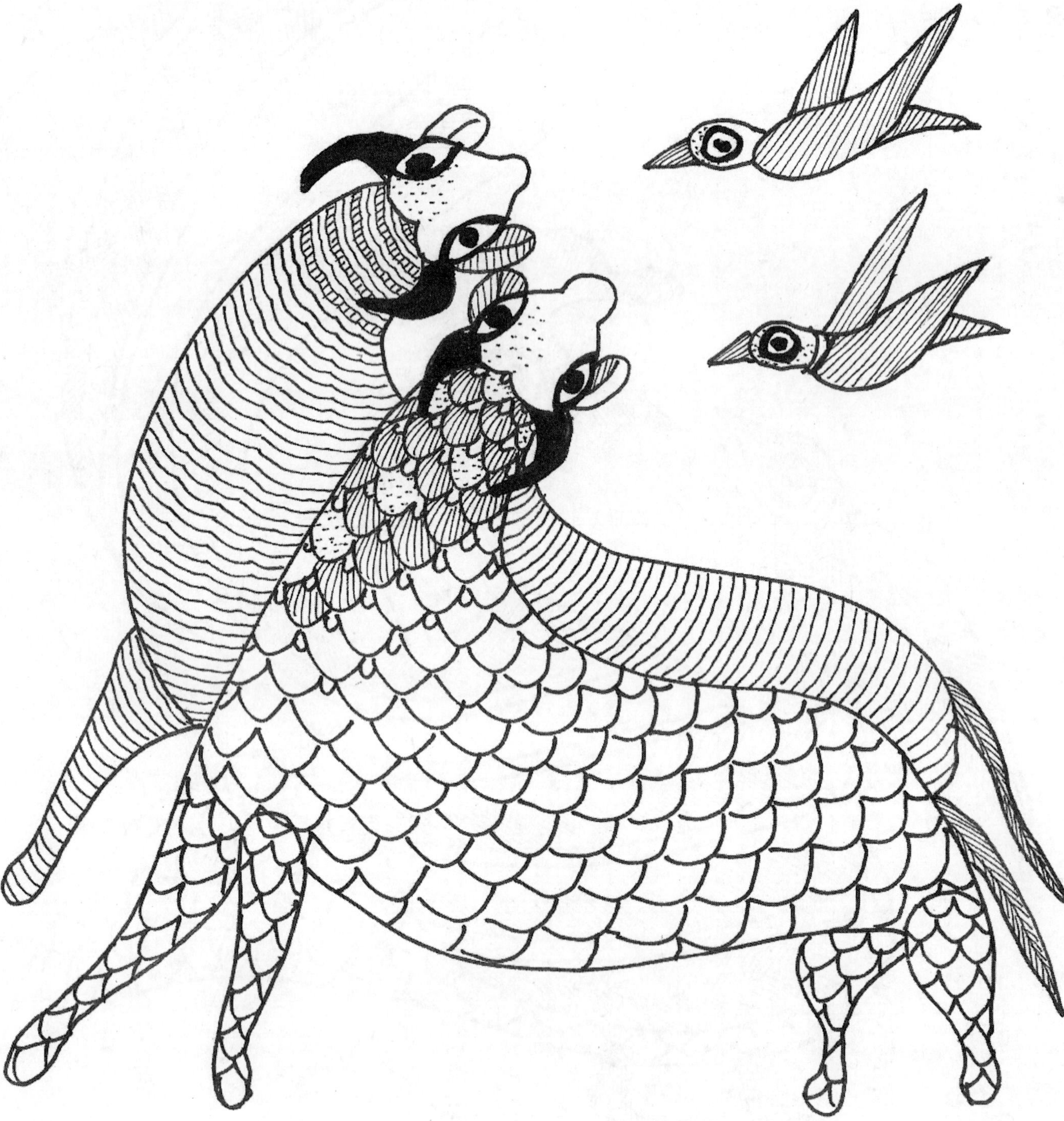

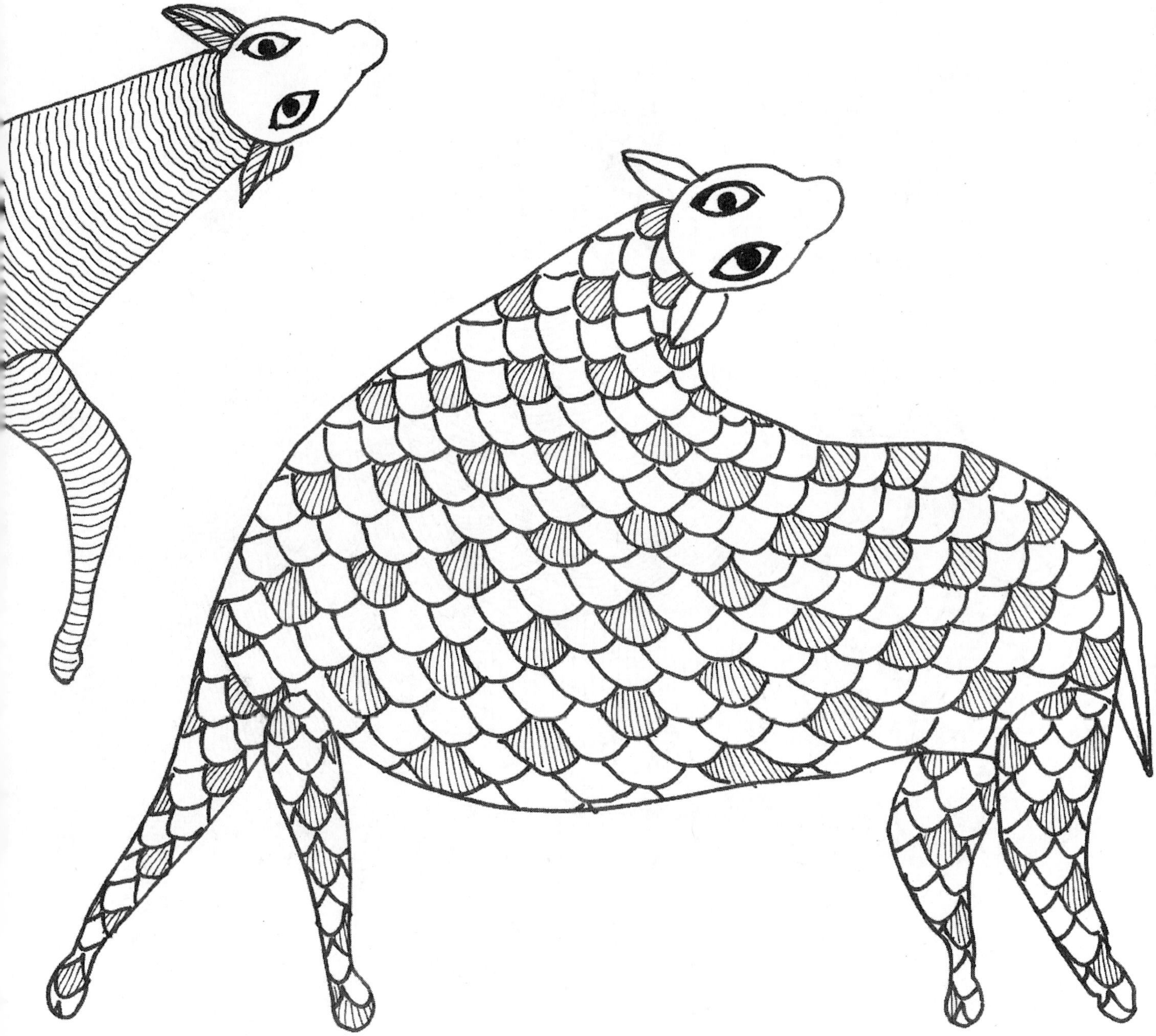

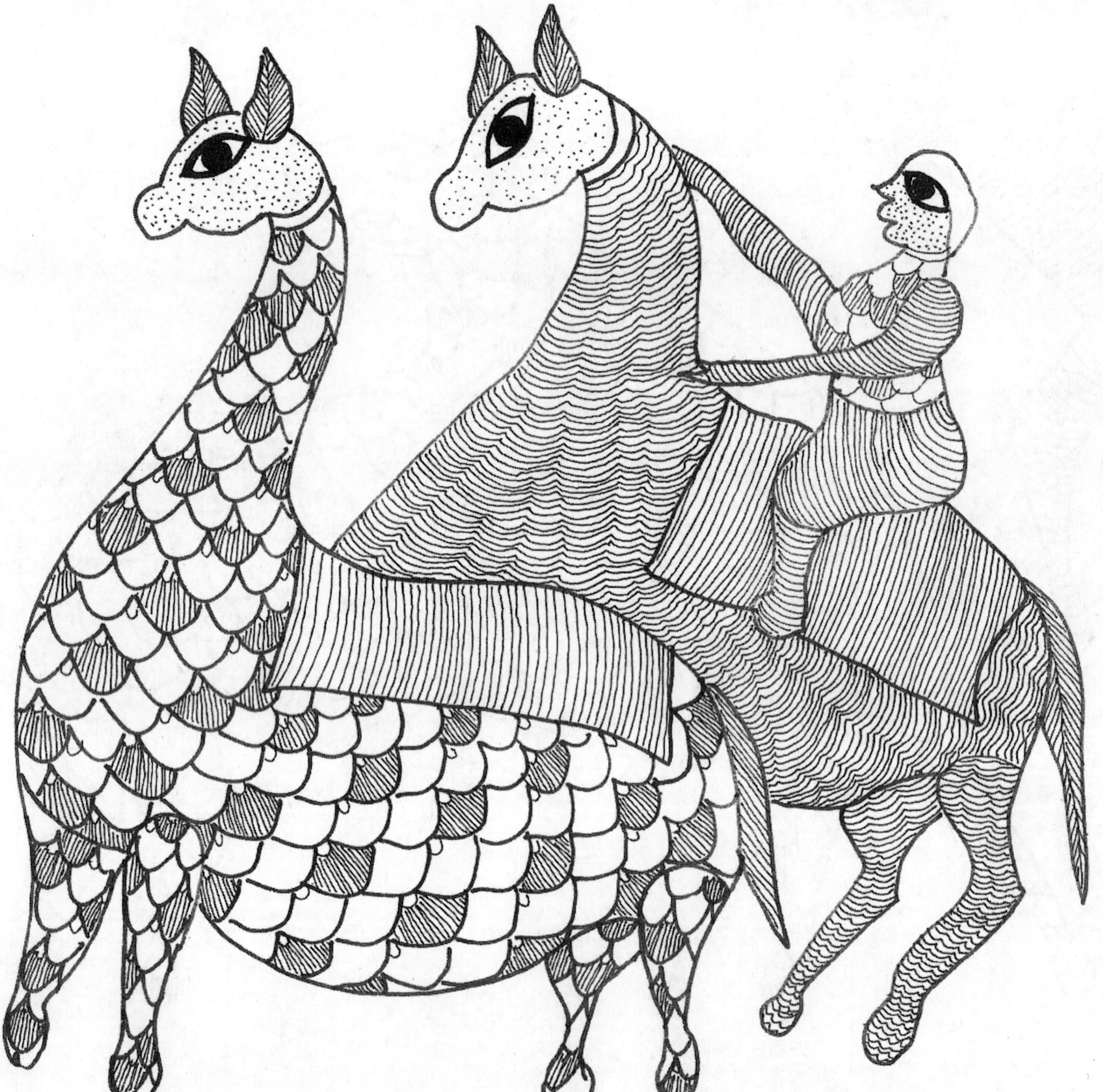

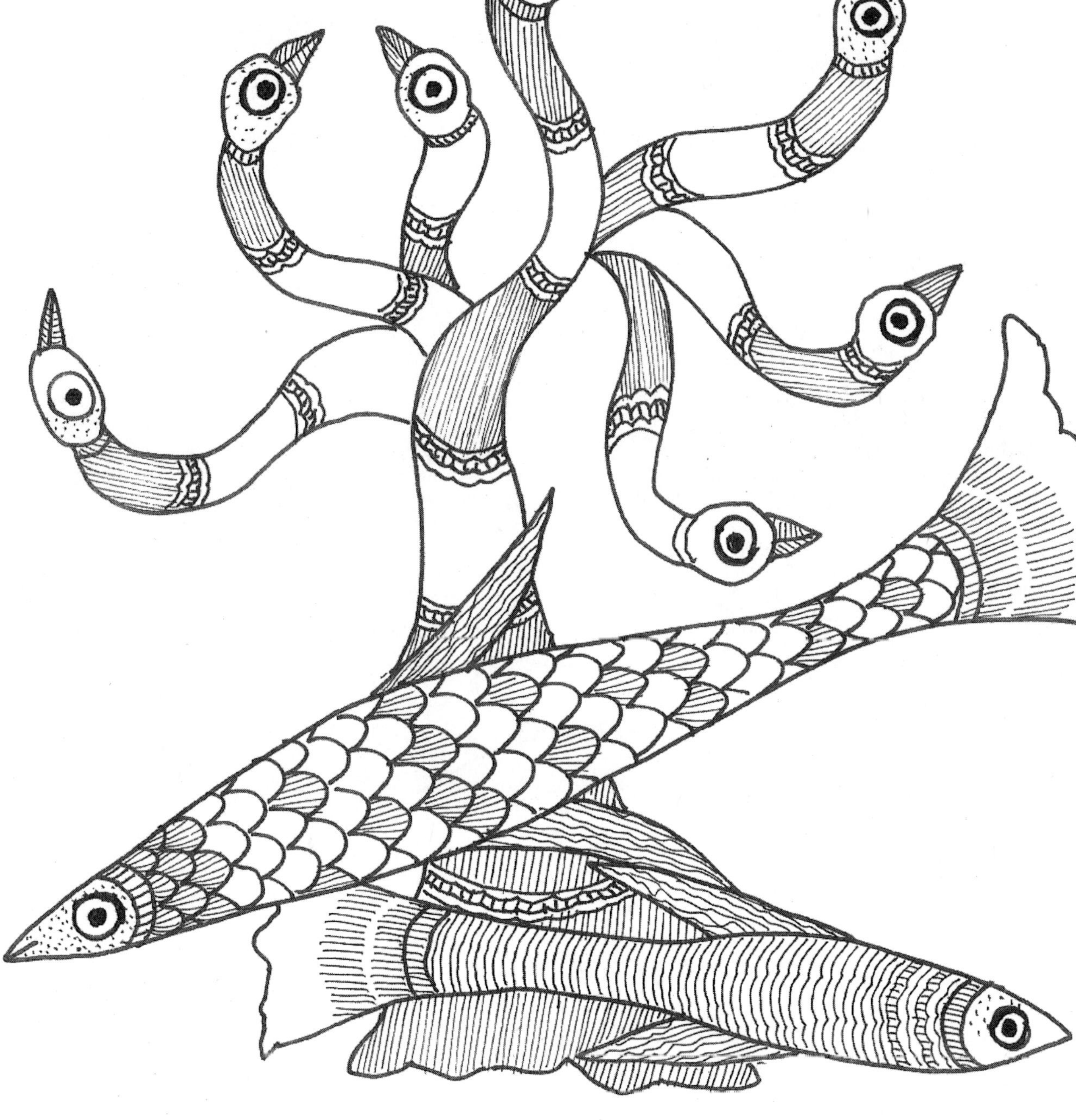

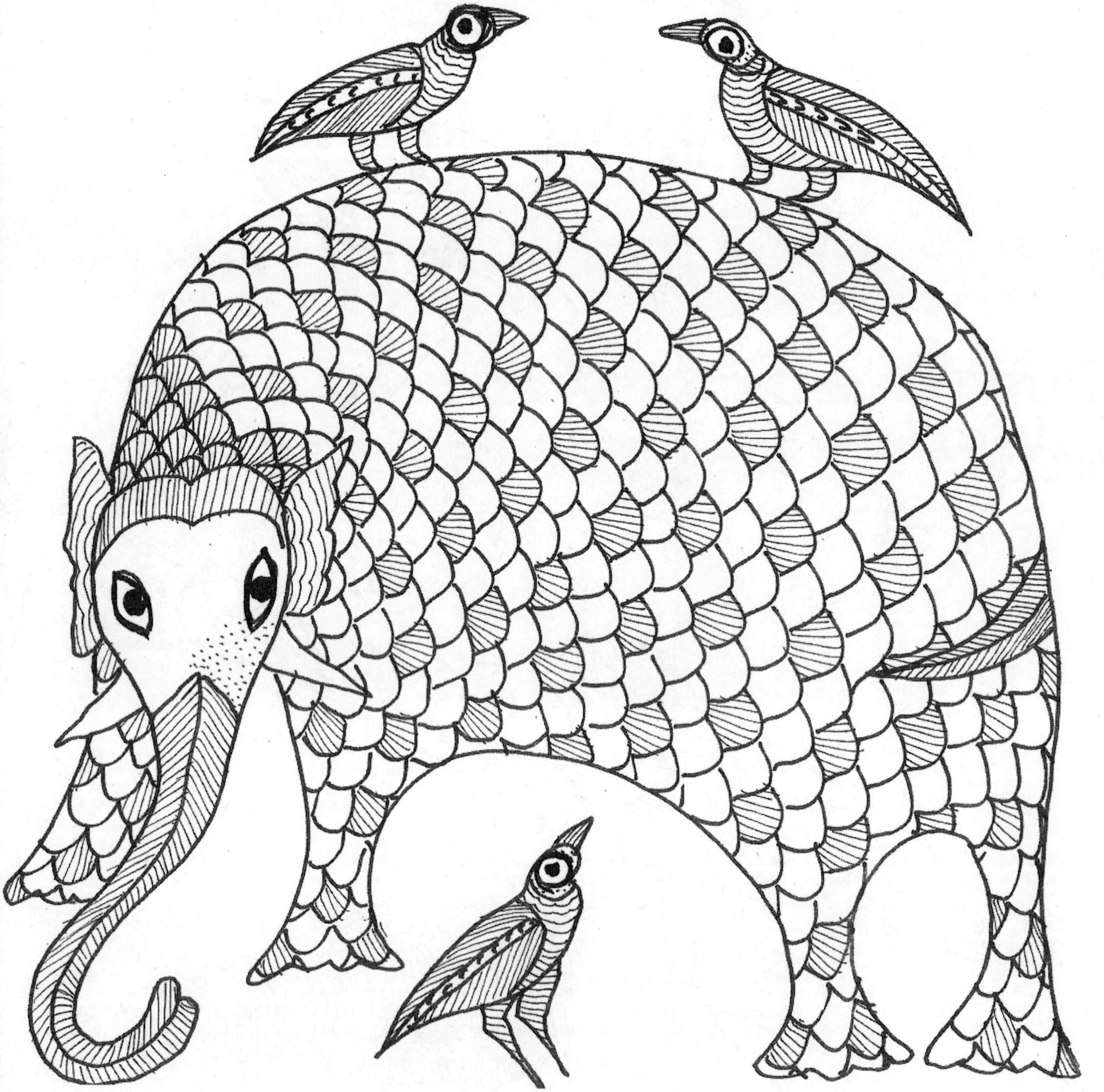

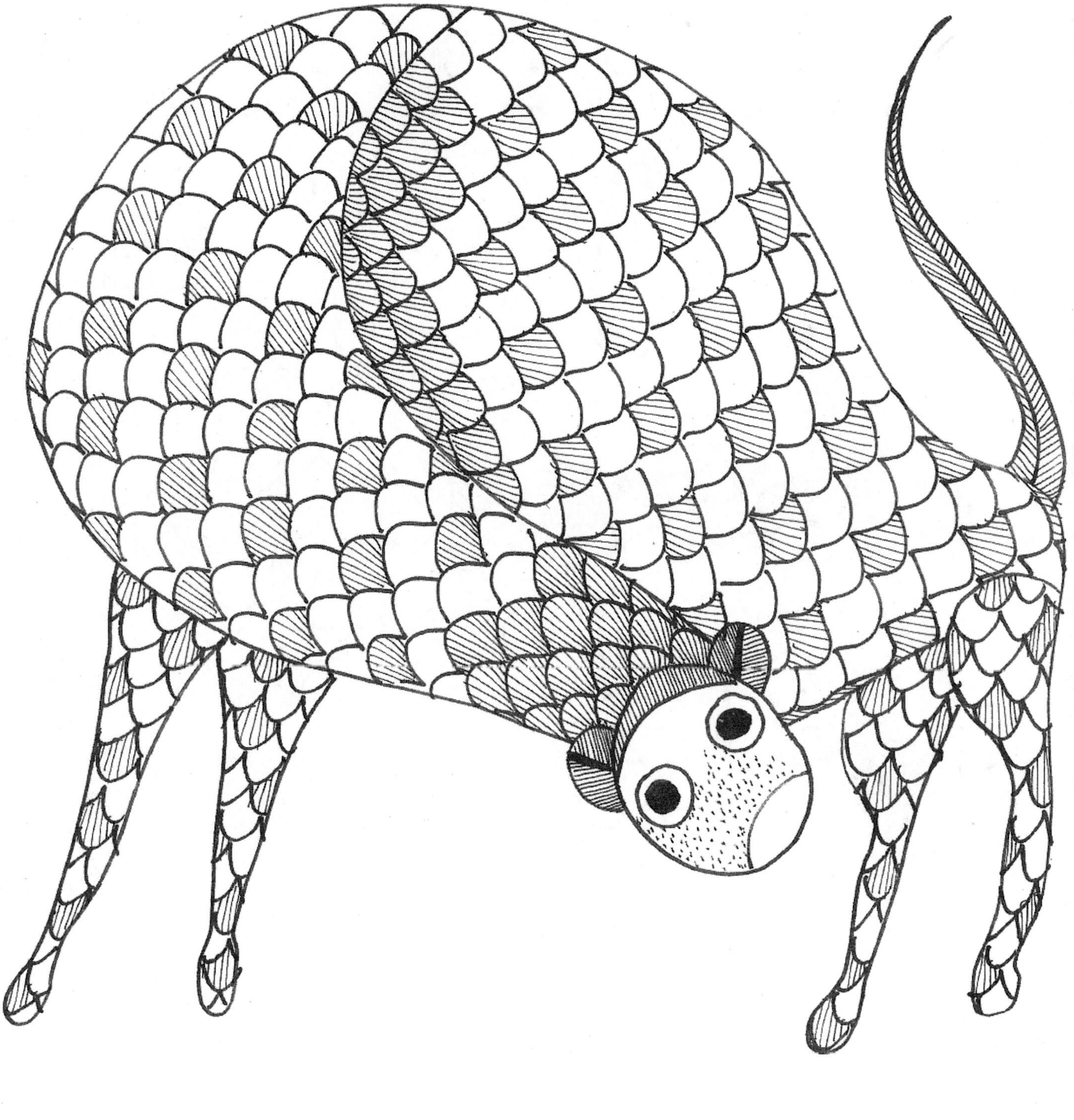

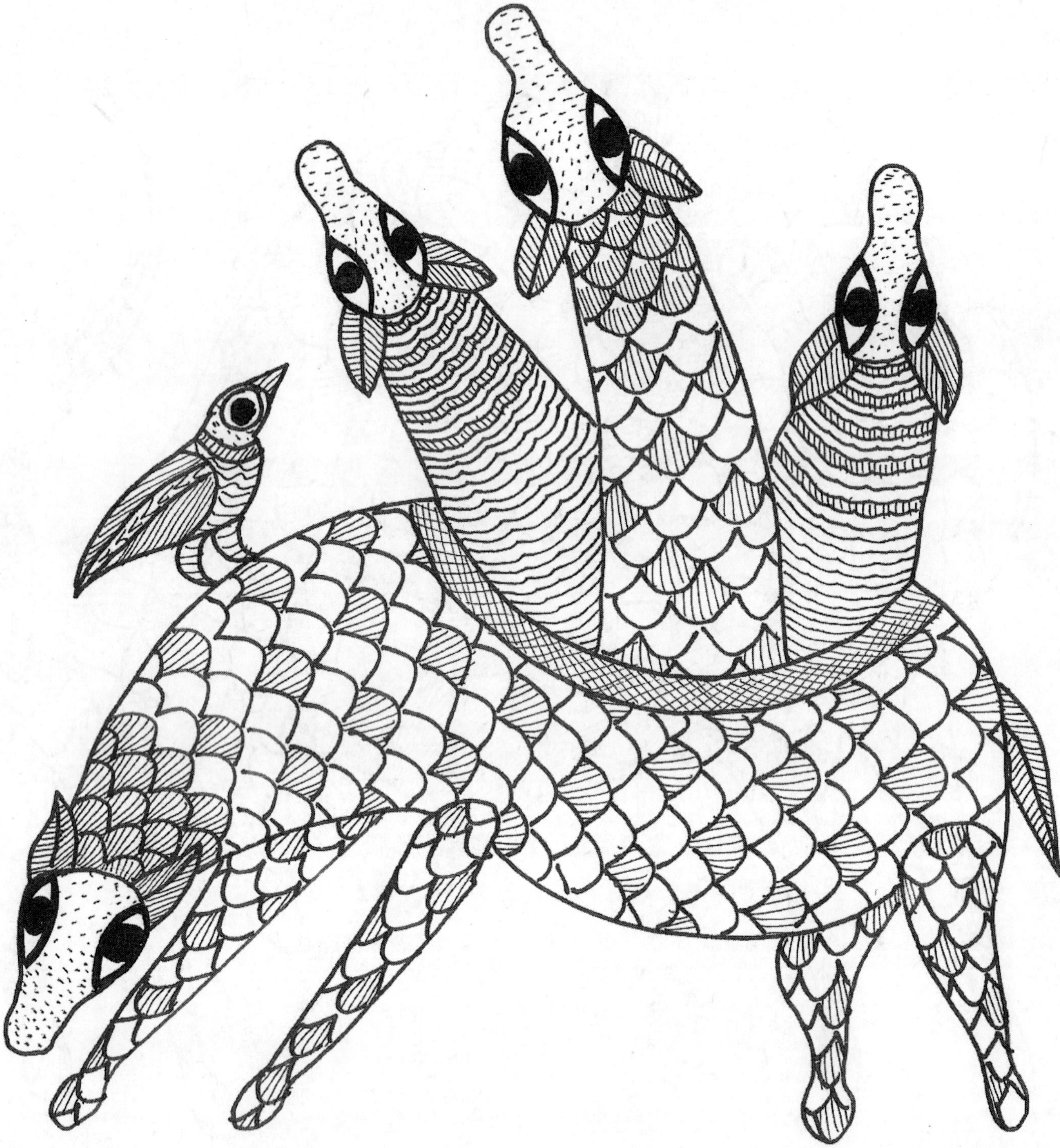

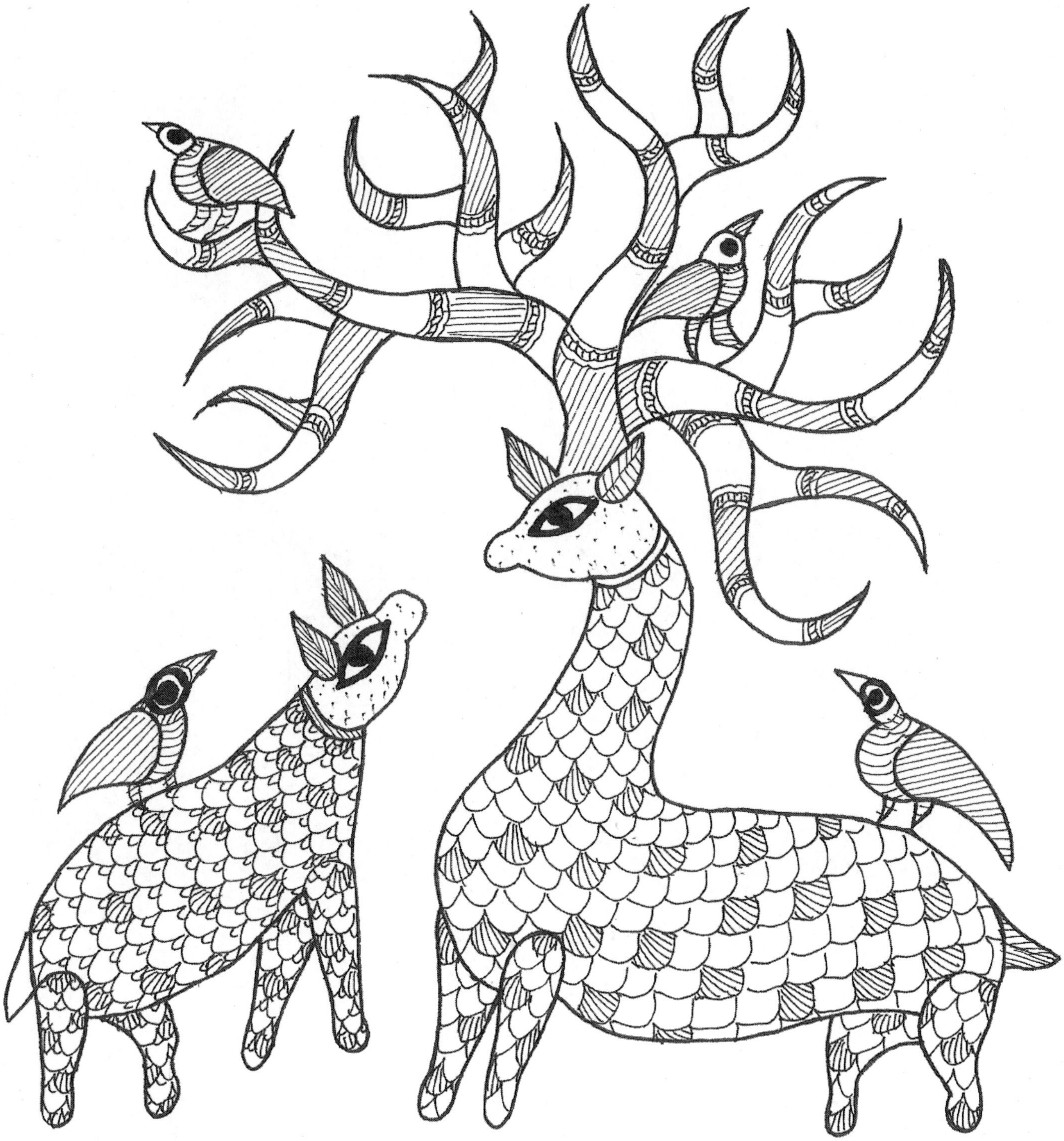

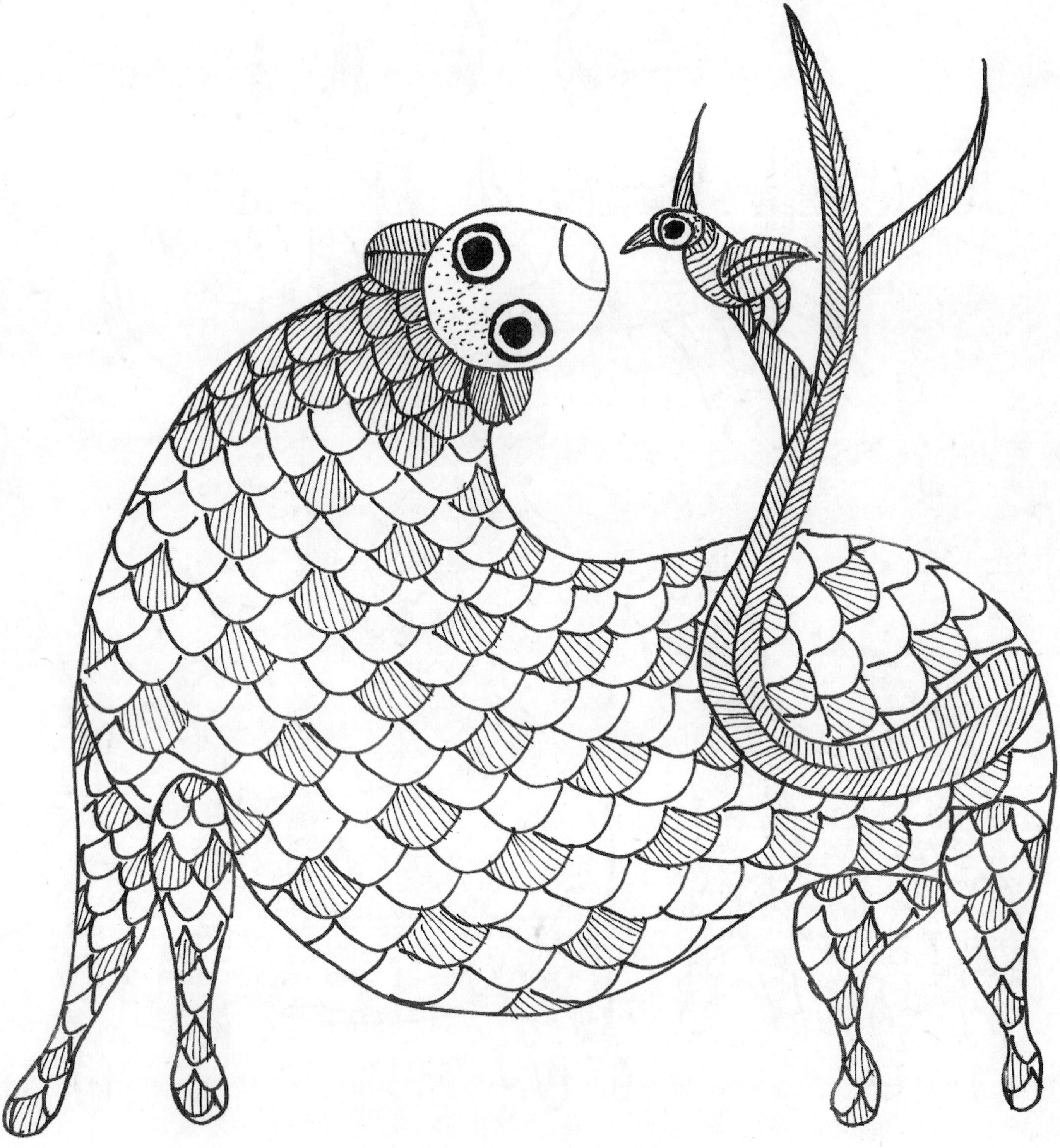

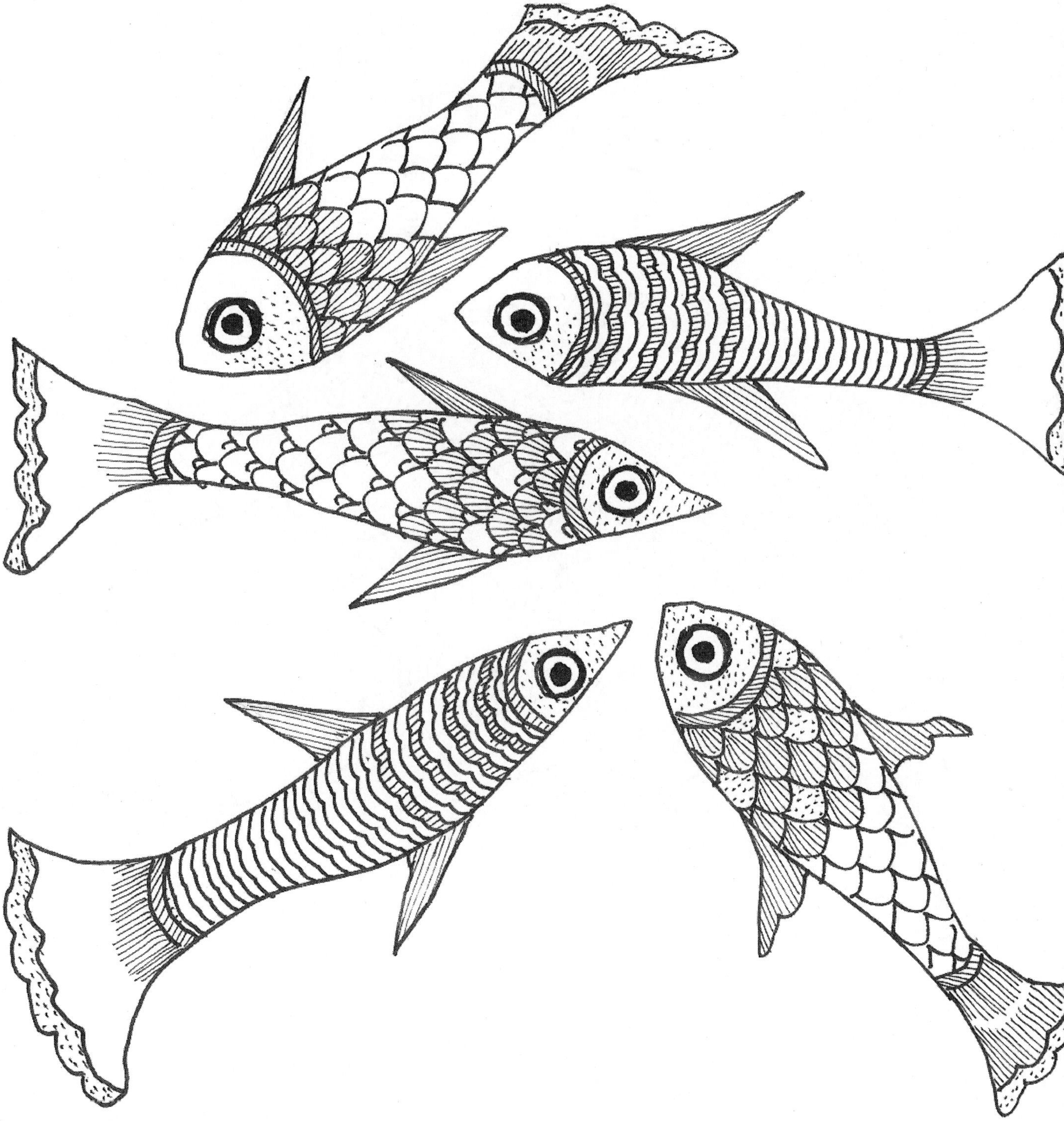

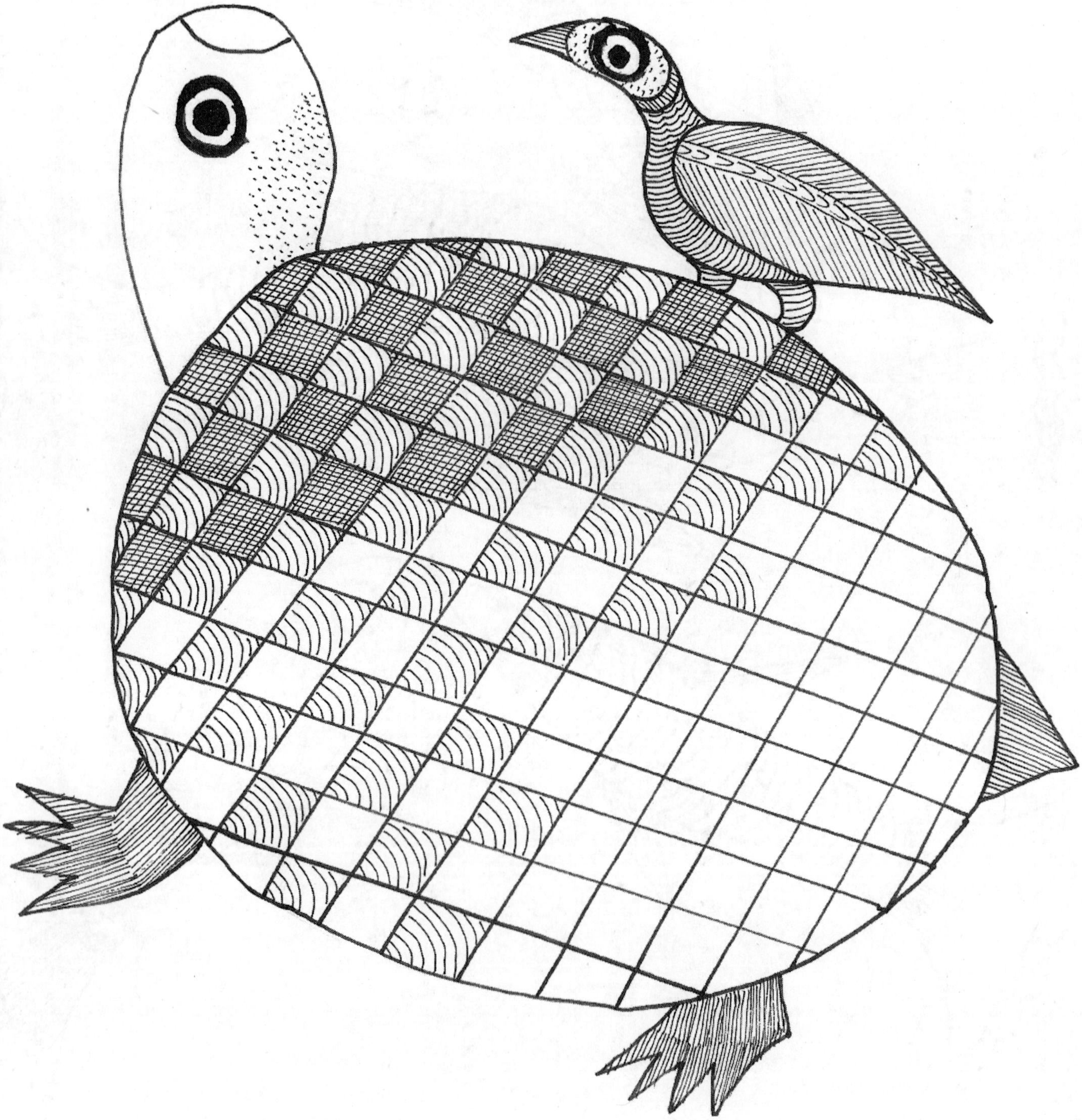

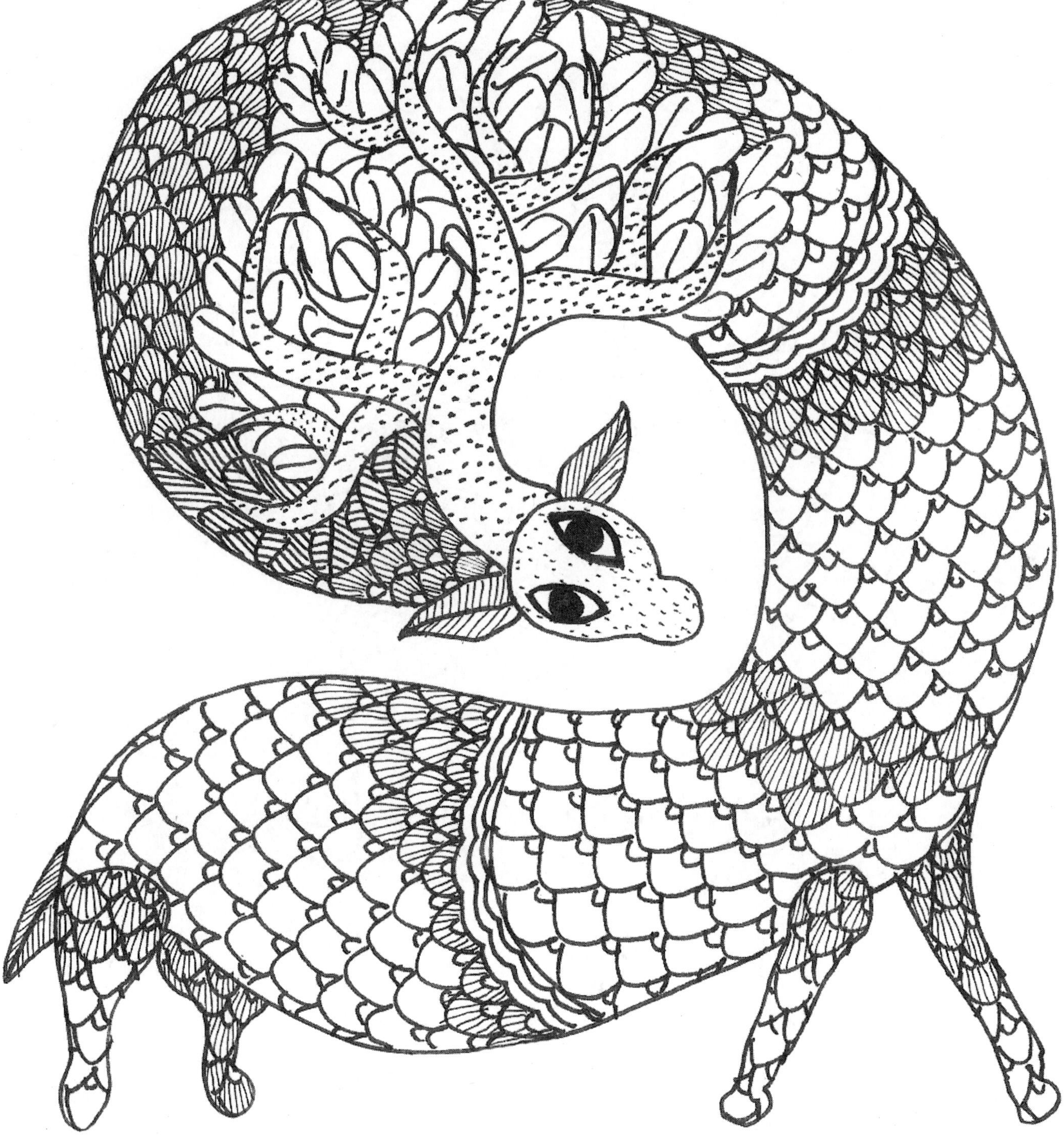

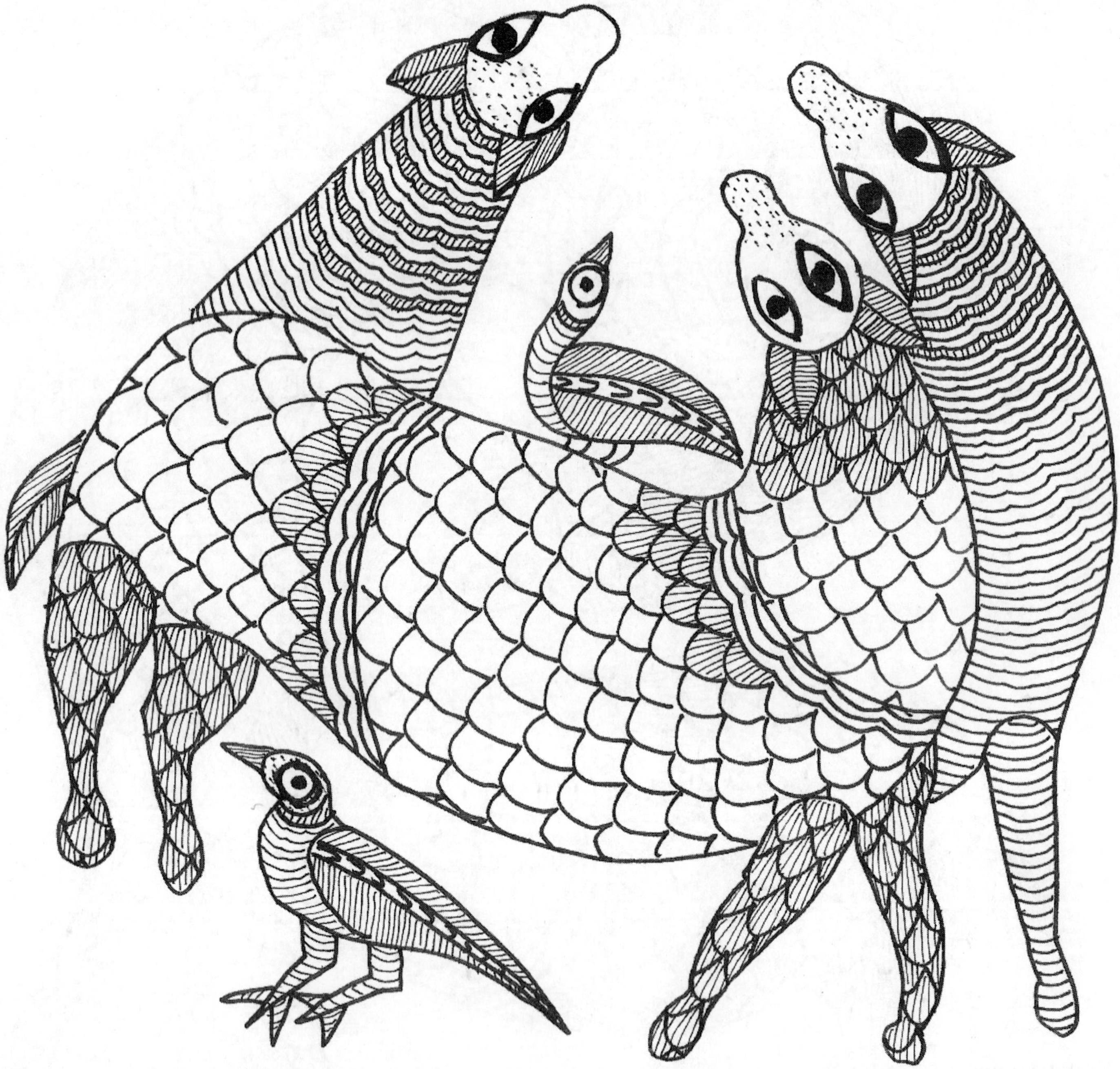

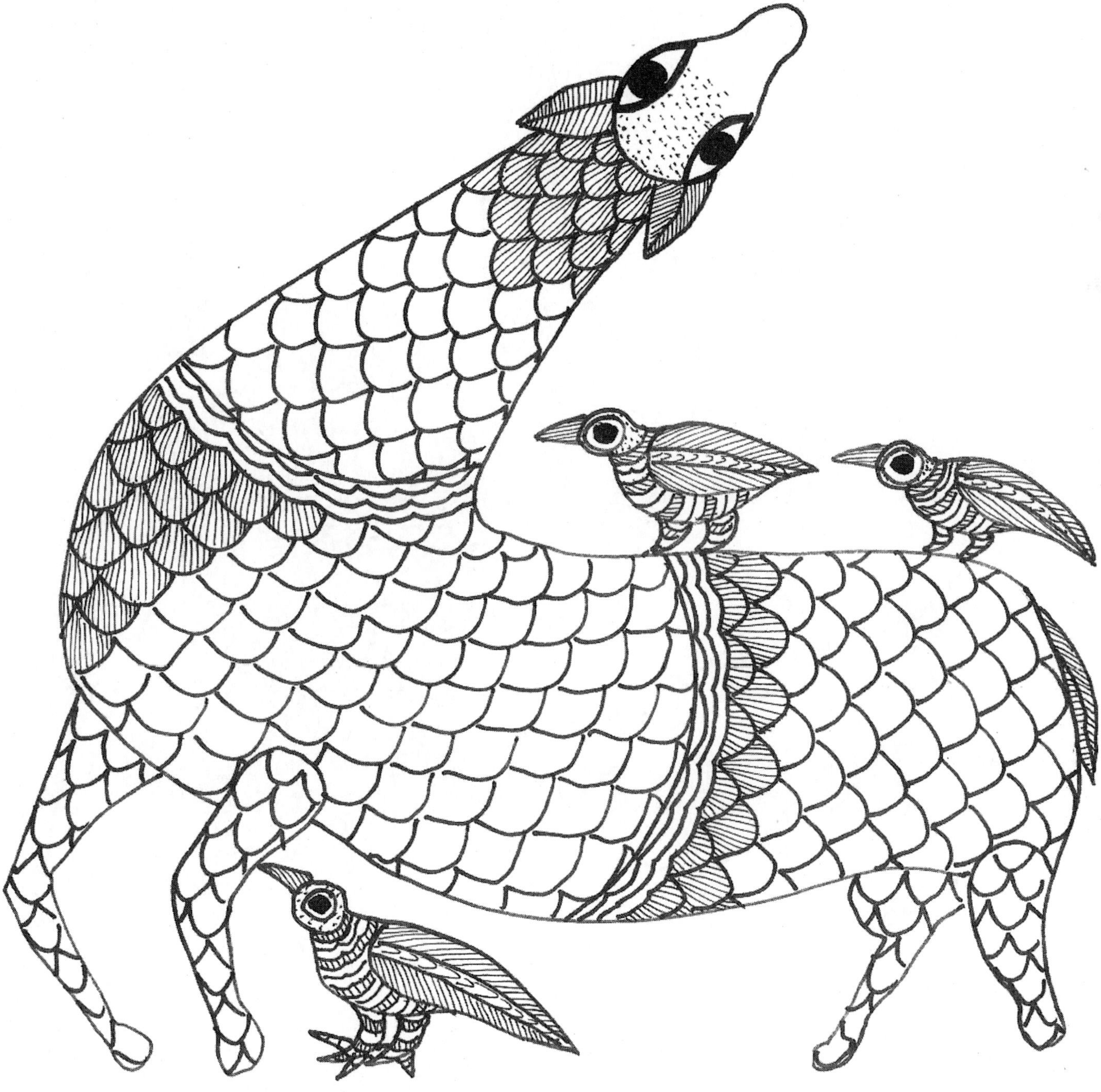

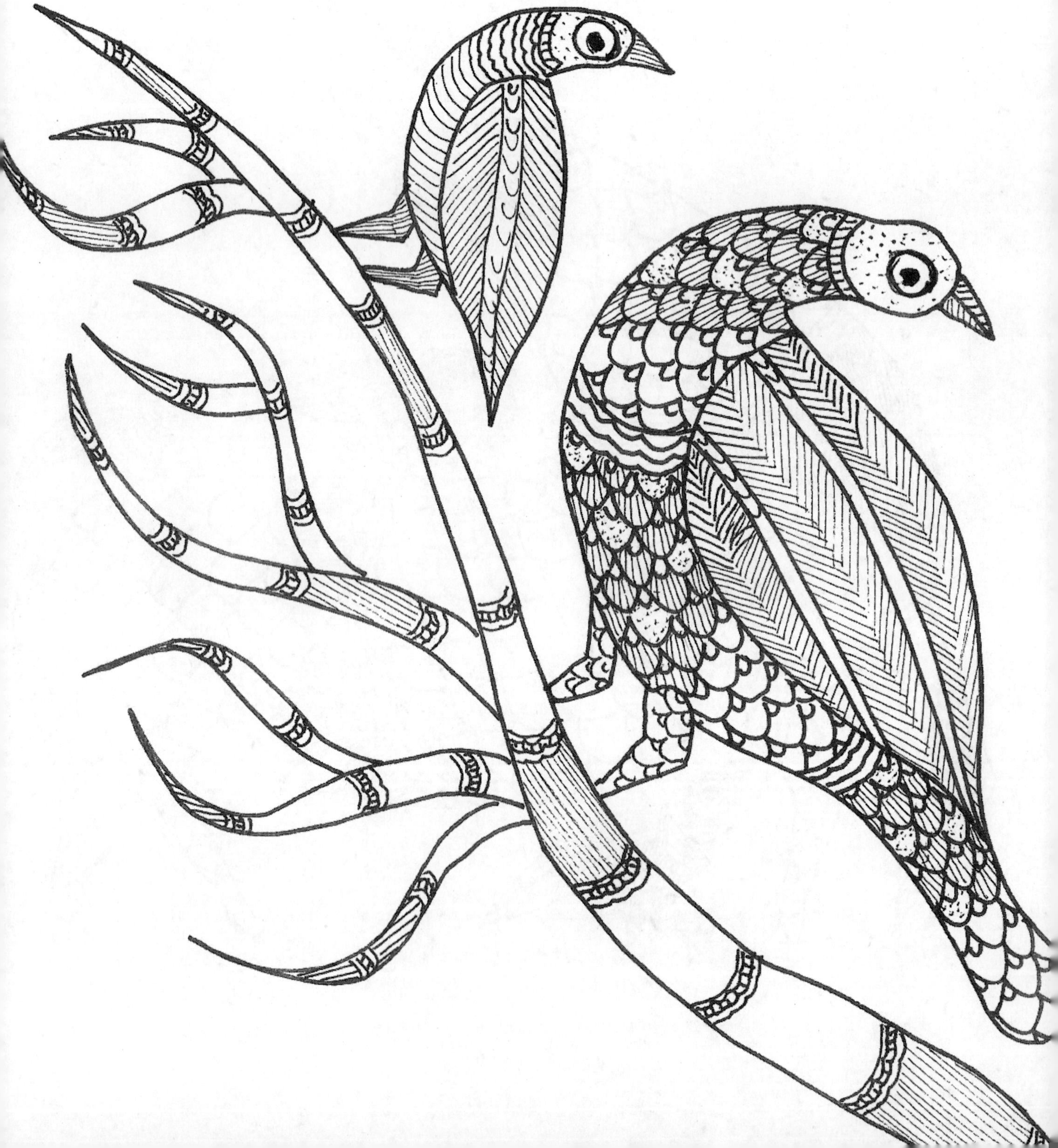

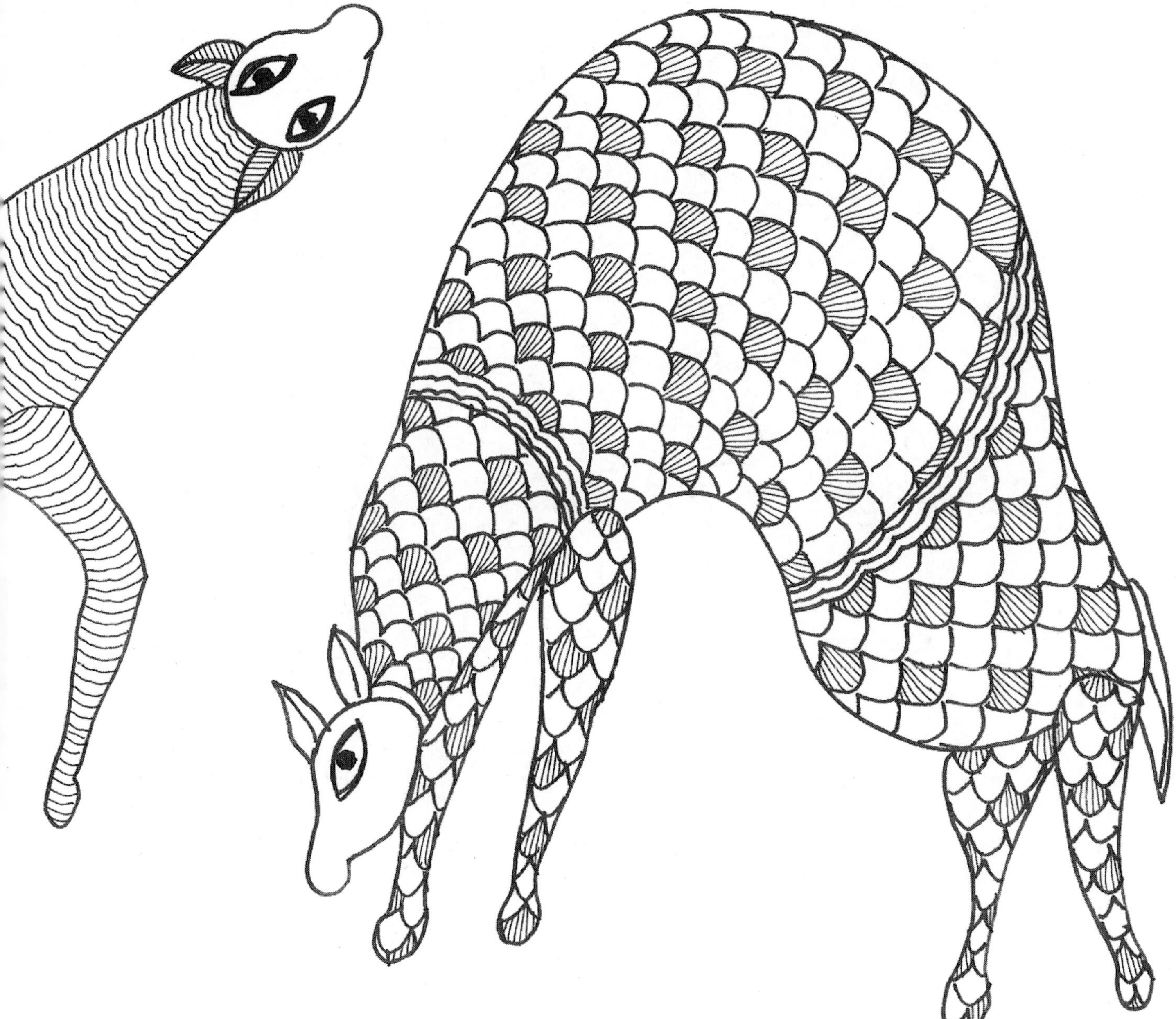

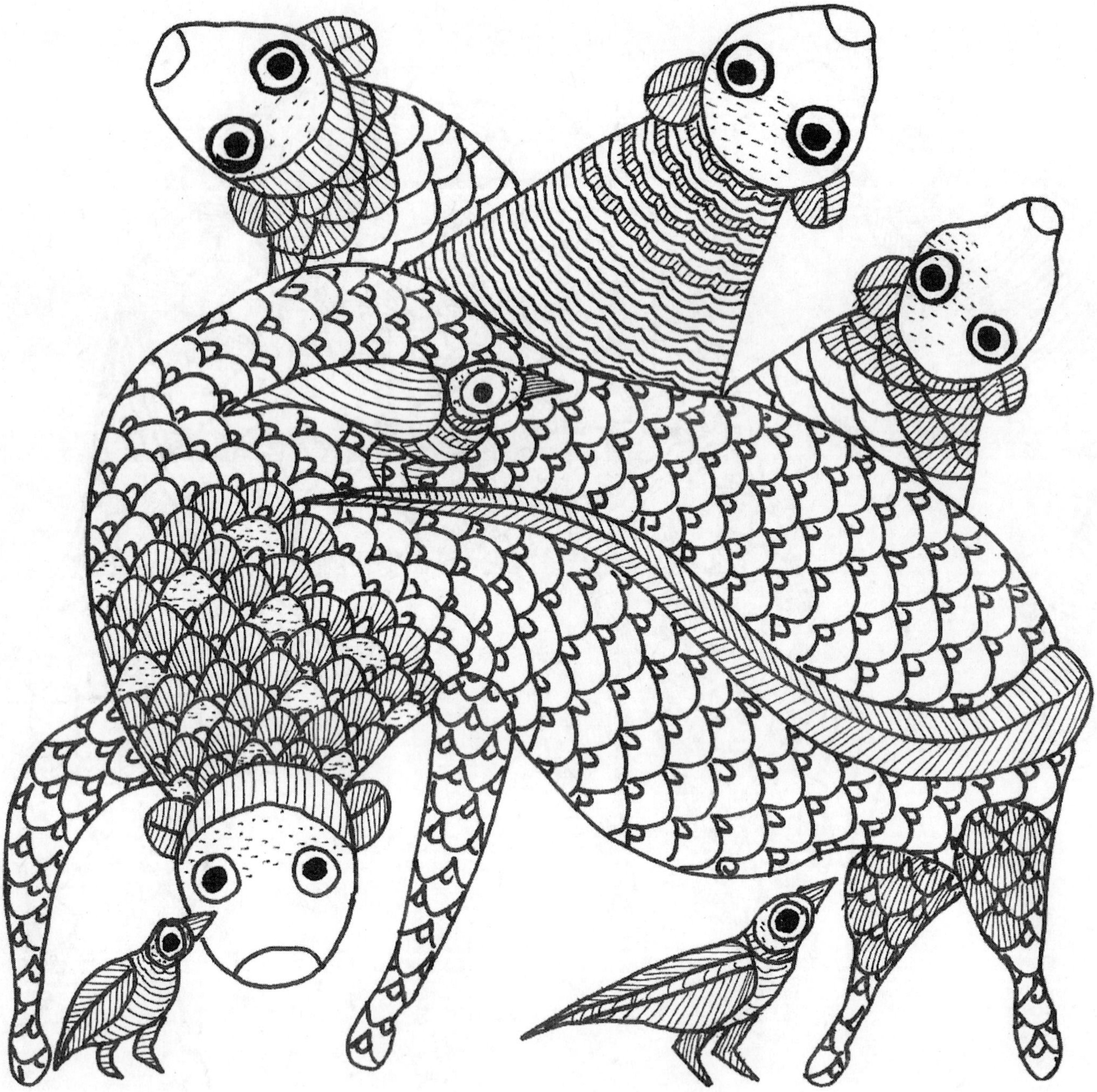

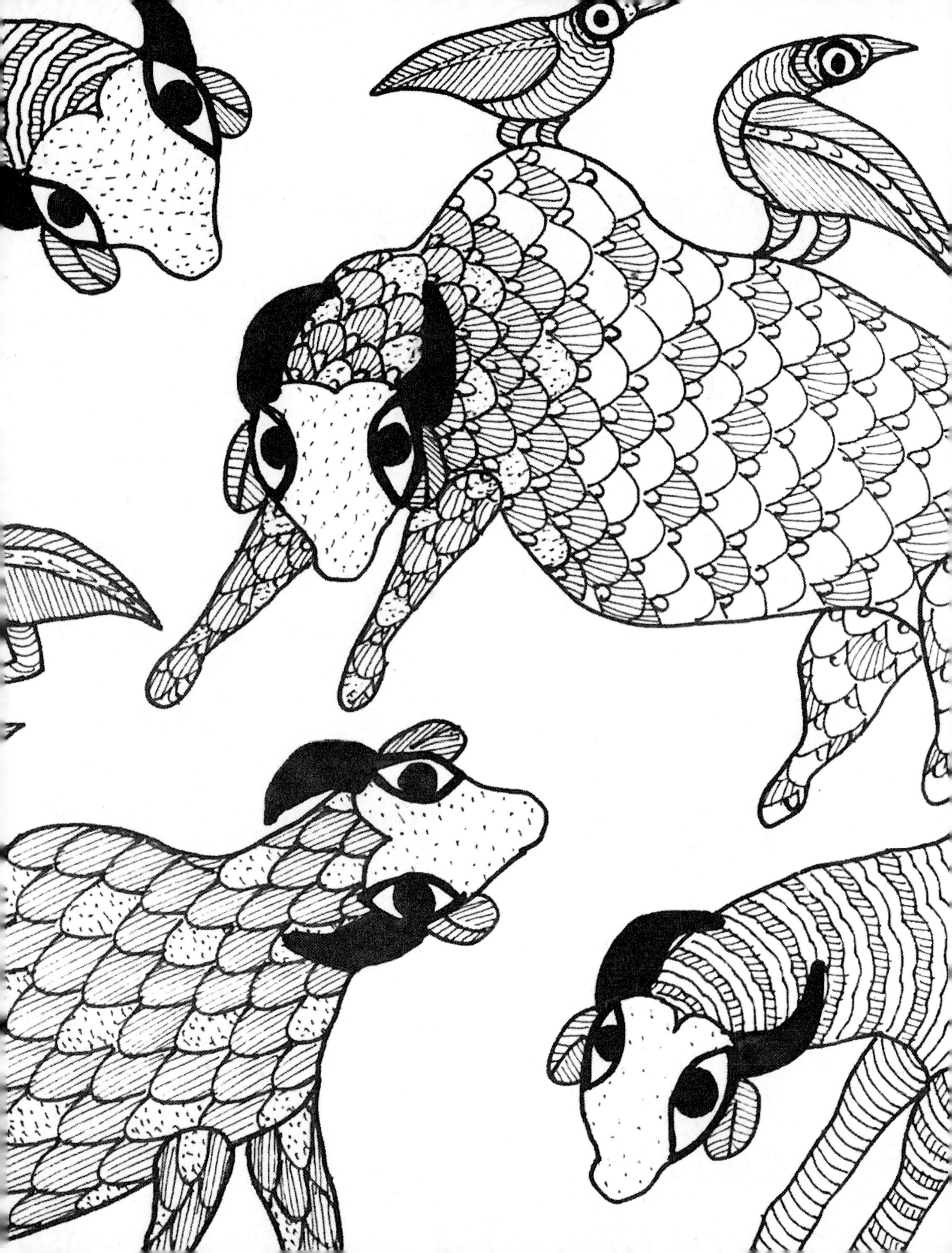

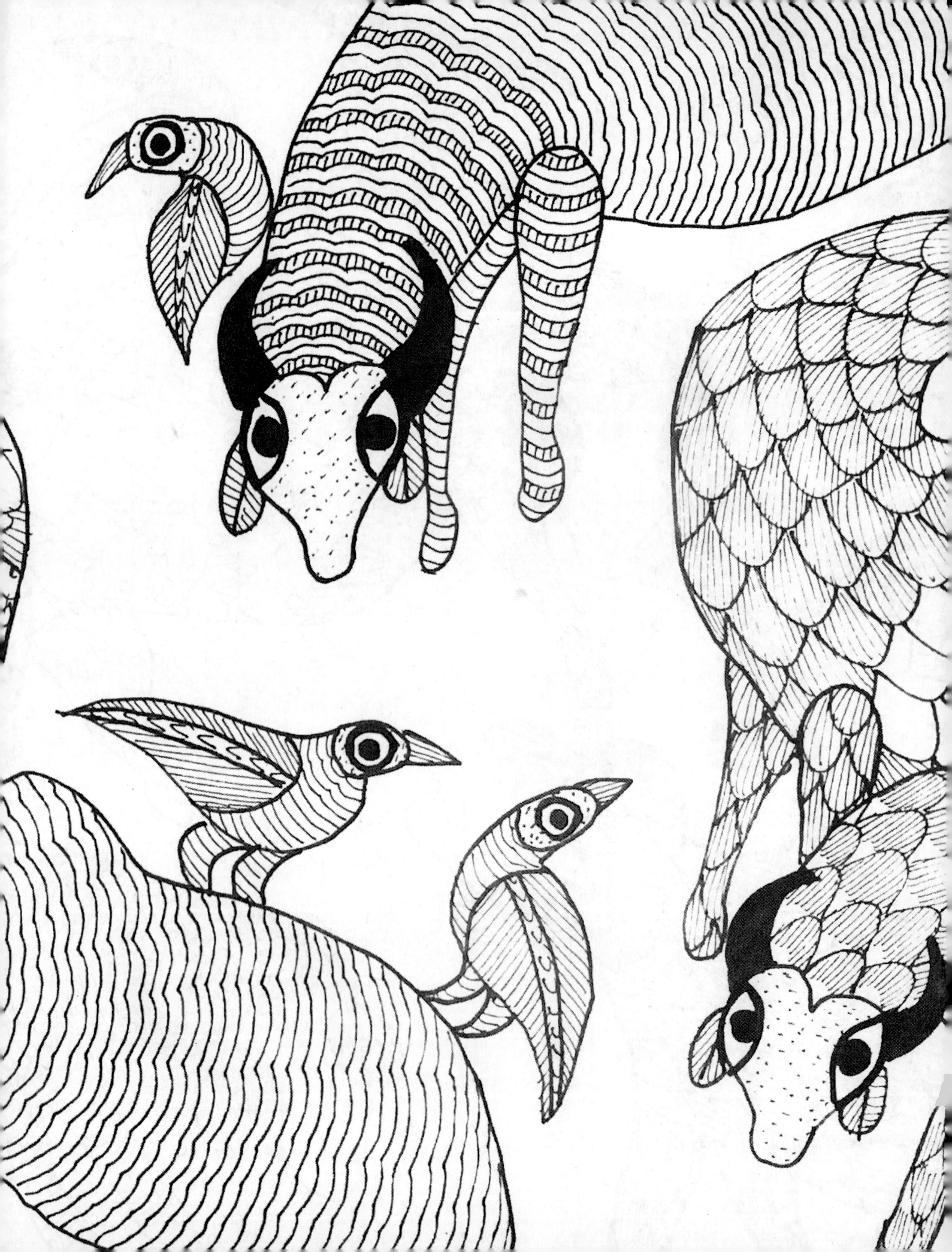

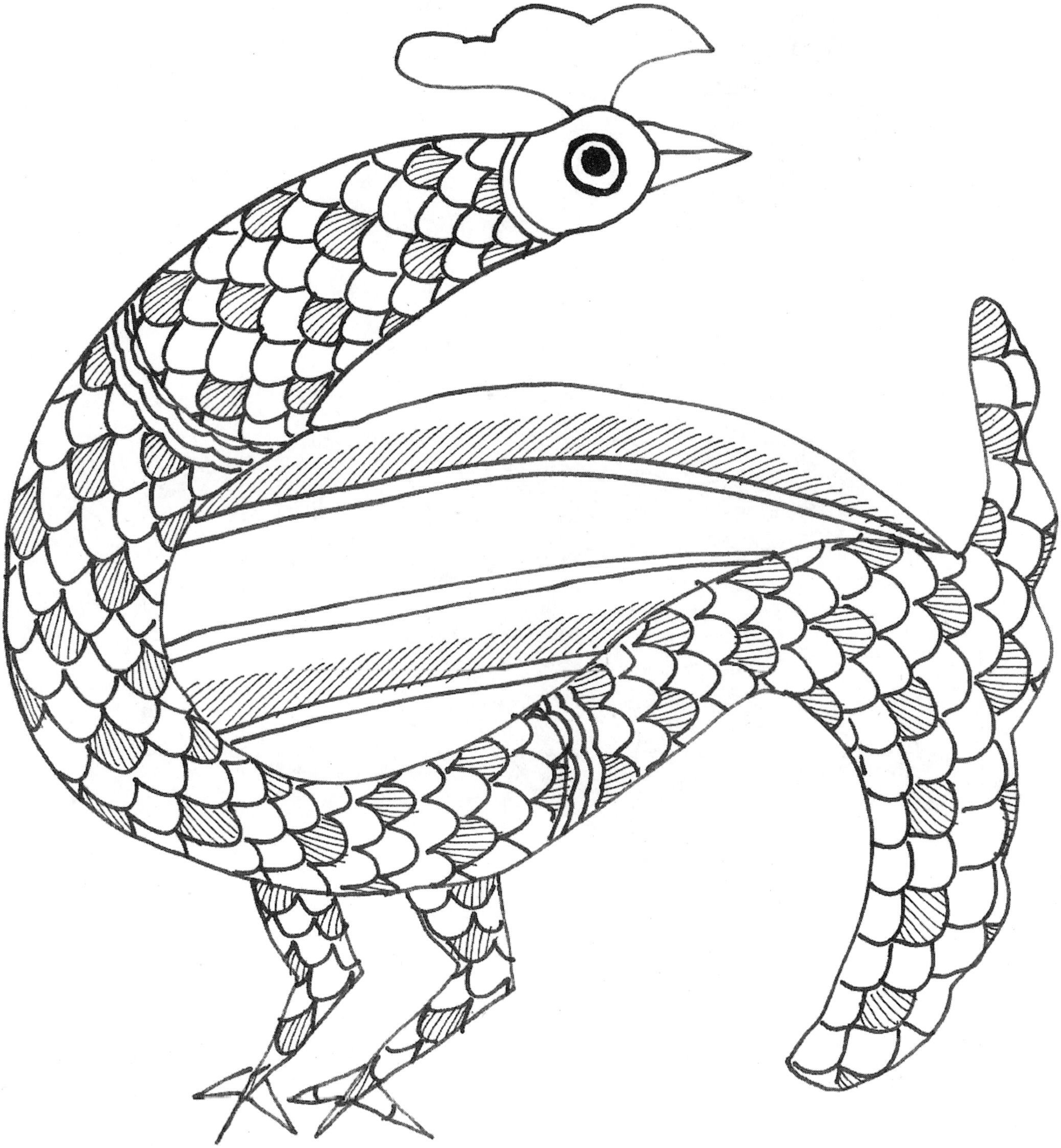

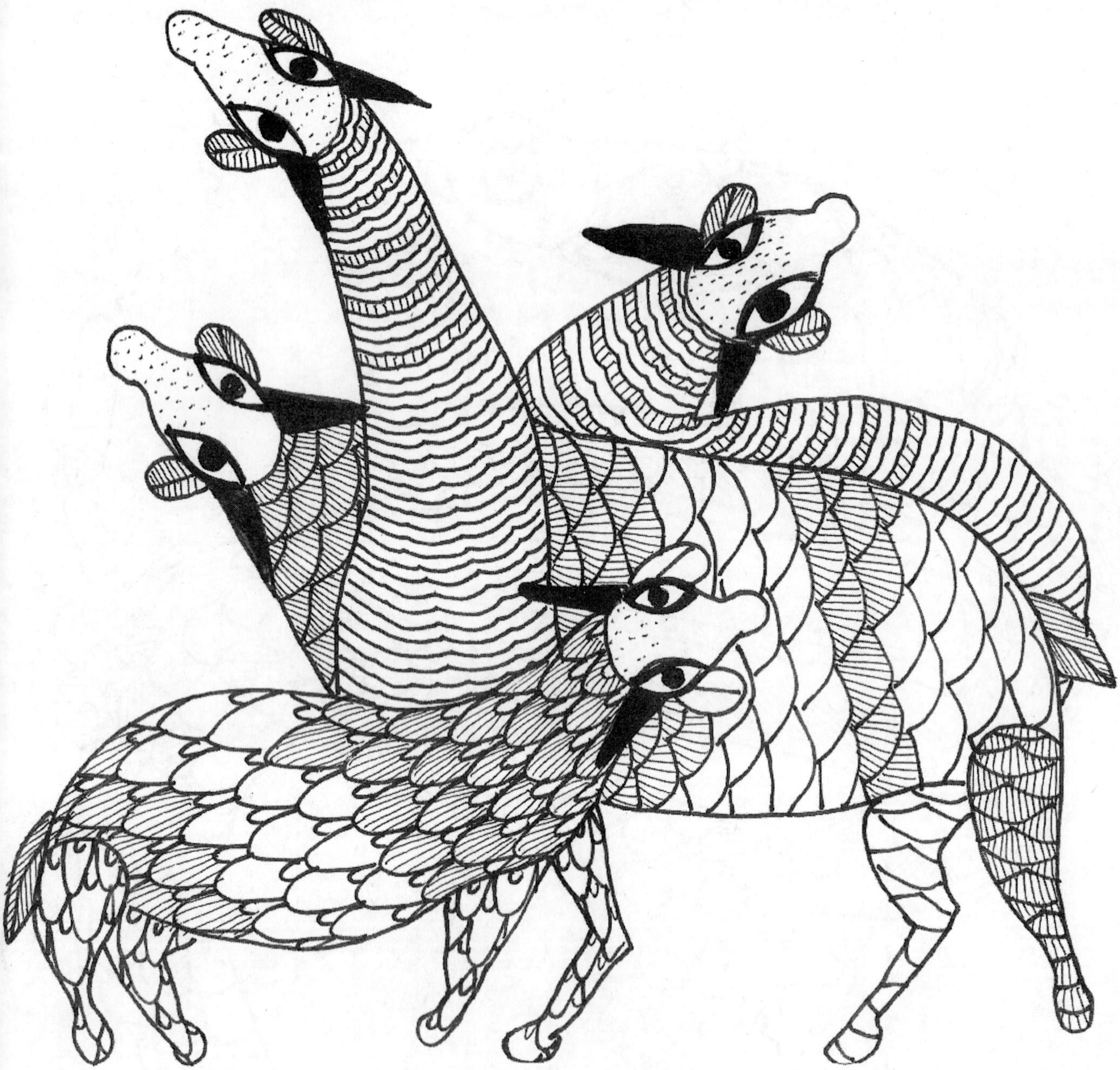

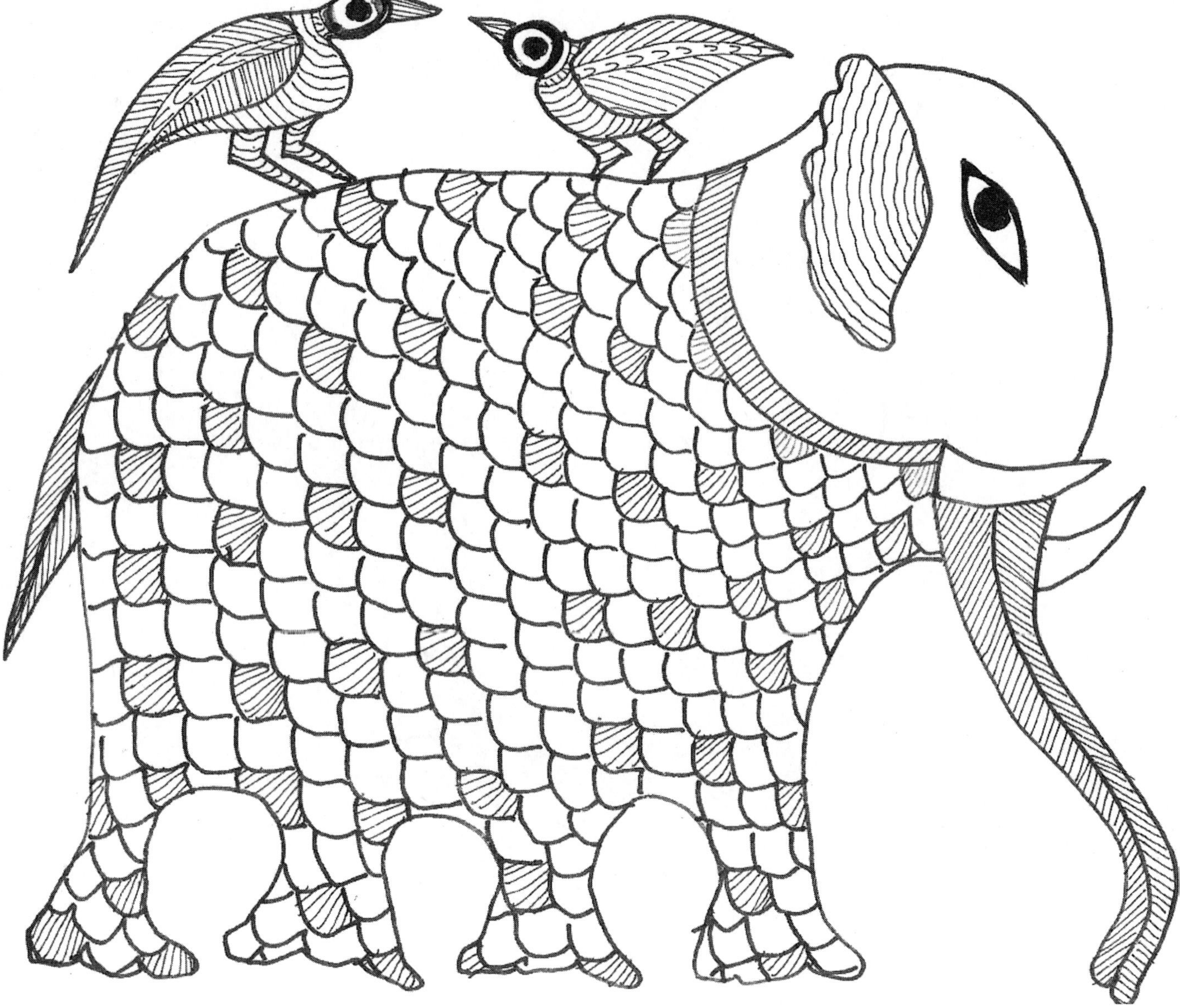

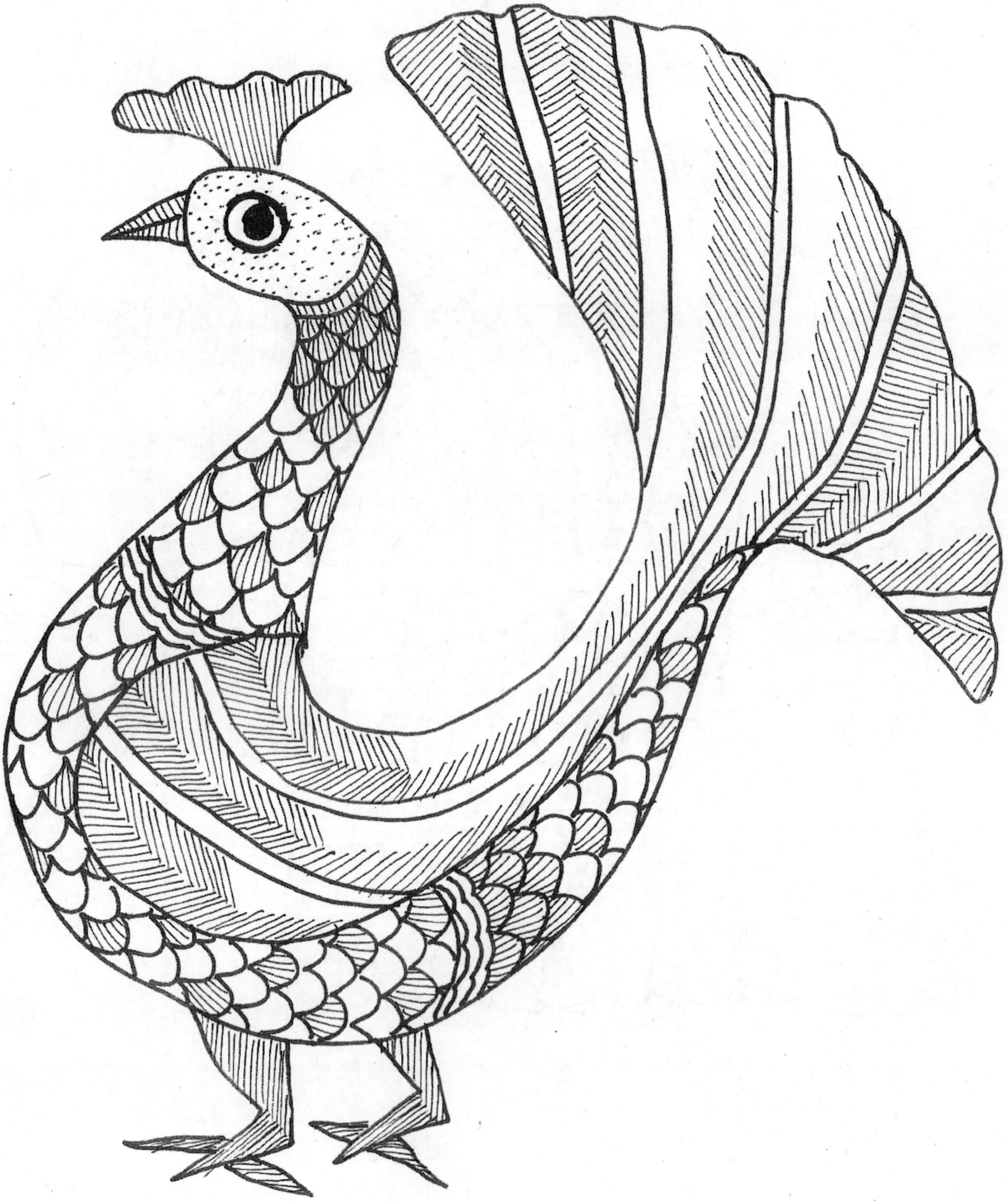

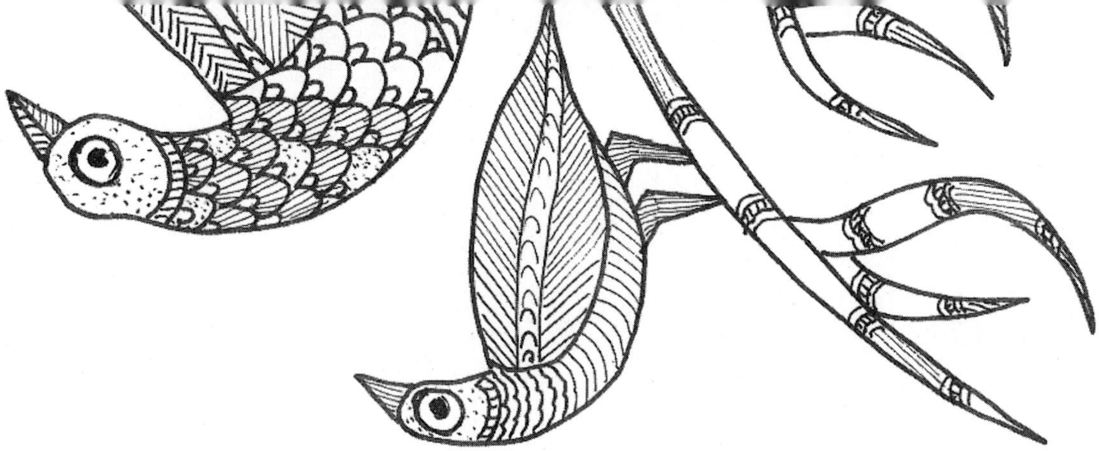

SUBHASH VYAM began as a sculptor before turning to painting. He was awarded the Rajya Hastha Shilpa Puraskar by the government of Madhya Pradesh, his home state, in 2002. In his recent paintings, Vyam has begun to depict characters and scenes from folktales narrated by his wife, Durga Bai, a renowned Gond artist herself. They have jointly illustrated the critically acclaimed *Bhimayana: Incidents in the Life of Bhimrao Ramji Ambedkar* (Navayana, 2011). Subhash Vyam lives in Bhopal, Madhya Pradesh.

BHAVI MEHTA is a freelance designer presently working out of her home studio in Pune. A graduate of the National Institute of Fashion Technology, New Delhi, she specializes in print design, books in particular. After her graduation, Bhavi worked with Penguin Books India from 2008 to 2013.

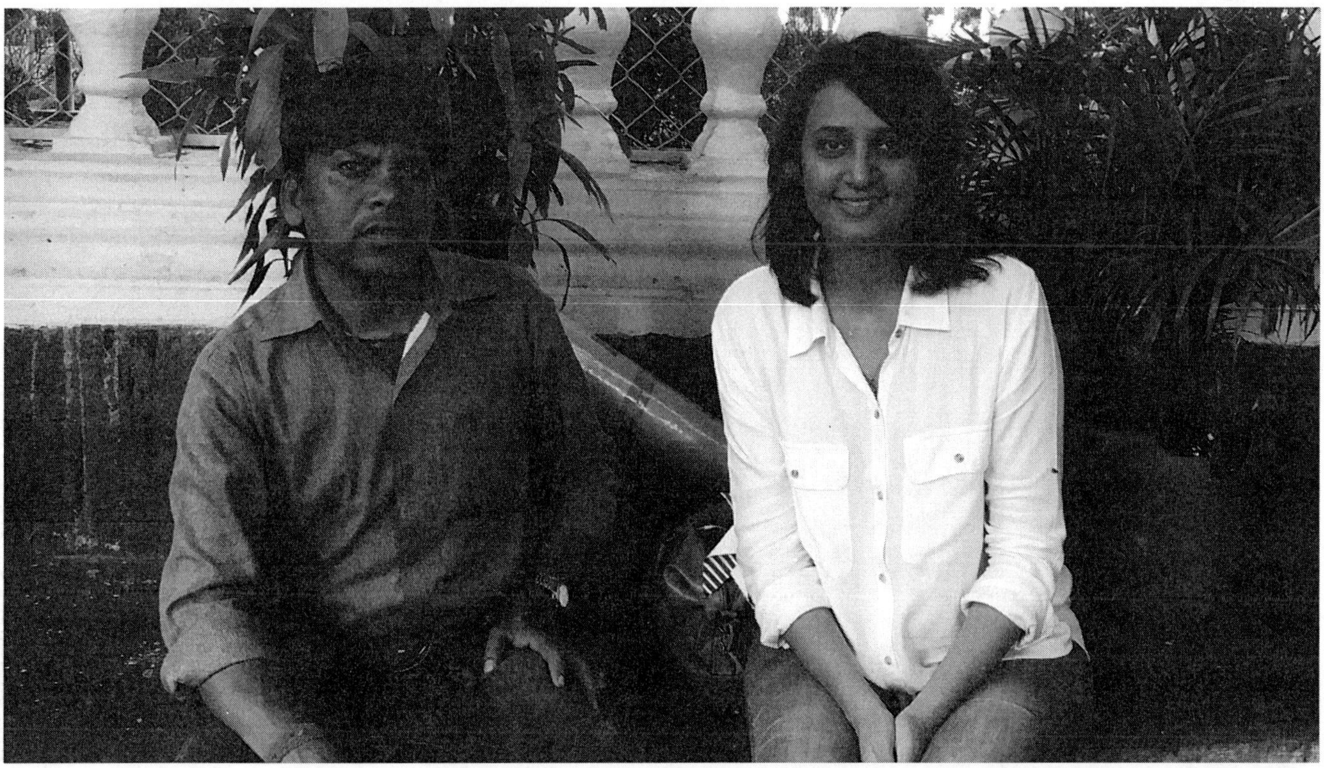